School Consultants Working for Equity With Families, Teachers, and Administrators

Bernice Lott and Margaret R. Rogers
University of Rhode Island

The aim of this special issue is to explore issues of equity within the context of school-based consulting with nonmainstream parents and their children. Ample evidence documents the difficulties faced by nonmainstream parents in the public schools in being respected as cocontributors to their children's educational achievement (Ho, 2002; Kozol, 1991; Nelson & Rogers, 2002), having their voices heard and welcomed by teachers and administrators (Christenson, Rounds, & Franklin, 1992; Fine, 1993), and getting their special interests recognized (Lott, 2001, 2003). This is especially problematic given research indicating that parental involvement in the schools is an important contributor to children's academic success (Heller & Fantuzzo, 1993; Henderson, 1987), classroom behavior (Comer & Haynes, 1992), and eventual school completion (Christenson, Sinclair, Lehr, & Godbar, 2001; Marcus & Sanders-Reio, 2001). Clearly, parents play a significant role in ensuring positive educational outcomes for their children so finding ways to facilitate their involvement needs to be a priority.

Working with school-based consultants is an important way that parents can interact with the schools to achieve positive outcomes. To date, the parent consultation literature has addressed an array of topics including parent consultation models (e.g., Sheridan, 1993), problem-solving steps used in parent consultation (Elliott & Sheridan, 1992), factors related to the effectiveness of parent consultation (Cobb & Medway, 1978), and home-based parent consultation (Edens, 1997; Greene, Kamps, Wyble, &

Correspondence should be sent to Bernice Lott, Department of Psychology, Chafee Center, University of Rhode Island, Kingston, RI 02881. E-mail: blott@uri.edu

Ellis, 1999). In a thoughtful analysis of the potential use of conjoint behavioral consultation with culturally diverse parents, Sheridan (2000) detailed the many ways the model has yet to be tested and pointed out the dearth of attention in consultation to nonmainstream considerations, issues, and populations. Indeed, very little attention has been paid to the work of school consultants as they negotiate between the needs of groups that have been historically marginalized and the constraints of public school culture.

We propose that school consultants have a major responsibility to recognize and then to challenge unresponsive and neglectful educational environments. Consultants can use their skills to try to effect positive change by reforming educational climates and services. We begin with brief discussions of diversity and equity, barriers faced by nonmainstream parents and their children, move on to the work that school consultants can do to promote equity, and then introduce the articles that comprise this special issue.

Each of the contributors to this issue has had experience working in schools with children and families from diverse nonmainstream backgrounds. Of the two guest editors, Rogers is a school psychologist who educates future school consultants, whereas Lott is a social psychologist. We believe that this combination has led to a dual but compatible perspective on the issues with which this special issue deals.

DIVERSITY AND EQUITY

The term *mainstream families* refers in general to families that are European American, middle class, Christian, two parent, one wage earner, heterosexual, and English speaking. The idealized mainstream model continues to be used by public educational systems as their cultural guide, despite the fact that in many parts of the country, such families are actually in the minority. Dual-wage families, for example, have become the norm (Procidano & Fisher, 1992; Smith et al., 1997), and stepfamilies are said to be "quickly becoming the family of the future" (Bray & Berger, 1992, p. 76). During the 1999 to 2000 school year, there were 18 million students of color in our country's 92,000 public schools, constituting 38% of the total number of students (National Center for Education Statistics, 2002a), "and almost 20 million (40%) students [were] eligible for free or reduced price lunches" (Maruyama, 2003, p. 654). A growing number of school-age students are linguistically diverse with almost 17% speaking a language other than English (United States Census, 2001). This is not surprising because approximately 40 million people in the United States speak over 120 languages other than English (Delgado-Gaitan & Trueba, 1991).

The families on whom we focus here span a range of ethnicities, social classes, religious backgrounds, national origins, occupational experiences, language proficiencies, structures, and sexual identities, because diversity extends far beyond ethnicity. There is a wide range of differences among groups that can be identified by social class, sexual orientation, and religion, along with diversity within them (Ingraham, 2000), and important similarities and commonalities as well.

Within the present context, equity means not only freedom from bias, but also the balancing of power for mainstream and nonmainstream families so that all families have equal opportunities within the schools, equal access to services, and share equal influence in decision-making processes. Equity for nonmainstream families means taking seriously the position, articulated by Weinstein (2002, p. 23), that "Schools function as door openers as well as gate-keepers for access to knowledge, and for meaningful participation in work and in the broader society." It is within the schools that human diversity can best be celebrated and utilized to expand and enrich both the process and content of learning.

The achievement of equity requires, as argued by Swadener and Lubeck (1995), that educators stop using the label "at risk" to refer to certain children and their families, and instead, regard all children and families as "at promise." In the schools, it is often assumed that being culturally different means being somehow deficient (Kalyanpur & Rao, 1991; Smith et al., 1997), and that nonmainstream parents are unreachable, difficult to communicate with, less concerned with and less valuing of education, inferior, and with little to offer to the education of their children (Edens, 1997). Such assumptions, Harry (1992) asserted, create barriers to the school participation of all but the most culturally mainstream parents and must be examined and eliminated.

Assumptions about "deficits," which are made about many minority or marginalized cultures, are victim-blaming and patronizing, and do not "address the structural evils, the corporate sins, and the broader social injustice" (Grant, as cited in Whitehouse & Colvin, 2001, p. 312f). Such assumptions have powerful expectancy effects that influence perceptions and treatment of nonmainstream children as well as the learning opportunities provided to them (Weinstein, Gregory, & Stambler, 2004). In writing about "lower track" classes in which Laotian immigrants were enrolled in one high school, Schramm (1994, p. 68) decried the deficit view of the students' abilities and experiences and an "administrative perspective…[that] reinforced their status as social and cultural marginals." Consider, for example, the following terms found to be used by teachers for students prejudged as unable to progress at the expected rate: *low read-*

ers, at-risk children, crack babies, lower-track, bussed in, and *from problem families* (cf. Metz, 1994).

Equitable treatment of the children and families of all cultural groups requires accepting and respecting their backgrounds and expecting that they can both learn from and contribute to what the schools offer. It means seeing families that are dissimilar from our own in some respects as quite similar in others and as connected to ourselves rather than as distant (Rodriguez, Taylor, Rosselli, & Thomas, 1997). It means learning about the barriers that nonmainstream families face when attempting to further the education of their children, striving to overcome those barriers, and delivering services on par with those delivered to mainstream families.

BARRIERS FACED BY NONMAINSTREAM PARENTS
AND THEIR CHILDREN

Inequities in our schools have been pointed to by many as presenting a major barrier to the success of nonmainstream children (e.g., Kalyanpur, Harry, & Skrtic, 2000; Pigott & Cowen, 2000). Calabrese (1990), for example, argued that it is the intolerant and discriminatory practices in our public schools that alienate minority parents and generate student problems such as dropouts, suspensions, failures, and behavioral difficulties. Indeed, within each of these problem categories we see disproportionate numbers of students of color and other minority groups represented. Among students ages 16 to 24, 27.8% of Latino students, 13.1% of African American students, and 6.9% of White students drop out of school in comparison to a 10.9% dropout rate overall (National Center for Education Statistics, 2001). Stanard (2003) suggested that the data drawn from the National Center for Education Statistics underestimate the problem and that other methods of analysis show that 46% of Latino, 44% of African American, and 22% of White students do not graduate from school. Students living in poverty are more likely to drop out of school than middle-class students (Streeter & Franklin, 1991), and among gay and lesbian youth, 28% drop out of school (Savin-Williams, 1994). Other research indicates that English Language Learners have one of the highest dropout rates of any group (Lindholm-Leary, 2000).

There are significant racial and ethnic disparities in suspension and expulsion rates in the schools. Data from the U.S. Department of Education as well as other sources (e.g., Center on Juvenile & Criminal Justice, 2000; Raffaele & Knoff, 2003) show that African American students are two to three times more likely to be suspended from school than are White students. One study found that when students of color engaged in minor infractions, the infractions were judged more harshly than when engaged in by White students, leading to differential expulsion rates (Morrison & D'Incau, 1997). These data suggest that the schools may be especially intolerant of and more punitive with minority students than mainstream students.

Nonmainstream parents and their children must negotiate relationships with professional educators and other school personnel who, for the most part, come from a different and more powerful culture. Recent data indicate that White teachers account for 90.7% of all educators, and teachers of color account for 9.3% (National Center for Education Statistics, 2002b). In 1999, the racial and ethnic breakdown of the world's largest professional organization of school psychologists, the National Association of School Psychologists, included 92% Whites and a combined 8% of Hispanics or Latinos, African Americans, Asian Americans, and American Indians (A. Hyman, personal communication, September 27, 2002). Many educators filter their interactions with nonmainstream parents and their children through the stereotyped beliefs and negative expectations they share with the dominant culture (Harry, 1992).

Research has consistently shown that many teachers have negative expectations for students of color (Dusek & Joseph, 1983; Garibaldi, 1992; Pigott & Cowen, 2000). Eighty percent of prospective teachers surveyed have negative attitudes about gay and lesbian students (Sears, 1991). Studies have found that teachers believe that African American children show higher rates of behavior problems (Zimmerman, Khoury, Vega, Gil, & Warheit, 1995), poorer educational prognosis (Baron, Tom, & Cooper, 1985; Garibaldi, 1992), and more negative qualities (Pigott & Cowen, 2000) than their White counterparts. Negative perceptions and expectations often translate into differential behavior toward students from different ethnic groups (Entwistle & Alexander, 1988; Wentzel, 1994). This can be damaging because we know that there is a connection between student engagement in learning, student academic achievement, and teacher involvement behaviors. Students who feel that their teachers are interested in them and concerned for their well-being are more likely to demonstrate academic success than are students who report low levels of teacher involvement (Tucker et al., 2002).

The behavior of school consultants may also contribute to barriers faced by nonmainstream parents. Kalyanpur and Rao (1991) and Edens (1997) described several consultant behaviors that discouraged the participation of ethnic minority parents in consultation. These include focusing on children's deficits, communicating distrust of the parents, misunderstanding the coping strategies used in environments the parents perceived as hostile, and using language considered insensitive within the context of the parent's sociopolitical history. Such behaviors serve to decrease parents' involvement and participation in consultations about their children.

Many of the parents themselves, if they have gone to school in the United States, have suffered the indignities of low expectations and discriminatory practices, that is, distancing and exclusion (Lott, 2001). Because nonmainstream school children do not "fit" the idealized White, middle-class model, they are likely to be regarded as "other," to be excluded from opportunities, and have fewer positive interactions with school personnel (Lott, 2002). Parents may have already experienced their own academic disappointments (Darling & Paull, 1994) and are now experiencing the increasing failure of their children. Low-income children, for example, show a decline in achievement and intelligence test scores from ages 7 to 9, and "the gains made...after Head Start and most other preschool programs are largely lost by the third grade" (Gersten, 1992, p. 151). This is a tragic state of affairs for the nation, but a heart-rending and humiliating experience for parents.

It is no wonder that research finds signs of alienation and withdrawal among some nonmainstream parents. Calabrese (1990) reported that parents of color differed from White parents in feeling unwelcome in their children's school and perceiving the school as hostile. They felt that "their interactions with teachers and administrators were dominated by the politics of confrontation rather than by...mutual respect or compassion" (p. 151). A case study of an unsuccessful effort to include a school in a large reform project revealed a number of serious problems, including cultural differences, perceived racism, and the feeling of dissatisfaction among African American parents about their lack of involvement in educational decision making (Meyers, 2002). In other studies, African American and Puerto Rican parents reported feeling that their interactions with school personnel revolved mainly around their compliance with procedural guidelines rather than meaningful interchanges involving a give and take of information about how best to educate their children (Harry, 1992; Harry, Allen, & McLaughlin, 1995).

Communication difficulties between school personnel and nonmainstream parents are not uncommon. Evidence suggests that some minority parents are initially satisfied when engaging in discussions about their children's educational placements but, over time, become disillusioned and increasingly nonparticipatory (Harry et al.,1995). Parents have reported impersonal, confusing, and jargon-filled communications often transmitted in writing, meetings scheduled at inconvenient times, and late notices for meetings. In addition, the existence of a power structure in meetings "in which professionals report and parents listen, implies that initiative and authority are solely in the hands of professionals" (Harry et al., 1995, p. 372). Such experiences tacitly communicate power differentials and can produce feelings of relative powerlessness and vulnerability for parents.

Communication difficulties may be compounded when both parents and school personnel hold preconceived expectations about each other's roles. Kalyanpur et al. (2000) described two problems that arise due to faulty expectations during special education deliberations that hinder communication and collaboration. Professionals are taught to believe that objectively derived knowledge is more valuable than anecdotal or subjective knowledge, and because parents do not share the same accumulated knowledge as professionals, parents are seen as less knowledgeable and informed. For low-income parents, their lack of "cultural capital" or "access to elaborate networks of support and [educationally relevant] information" (p. 126) places them at a distinct disadvantage in successfully negotiating the channels within the educational system (Kalyanpur et al., 2000). Parents are expected to share in the decision-making process about their children's education, but, because their knowledge is devalued, it is likely to be dismissed more readily than professional input, rendering parental input less influential and persuasive in deliberations. Astute parents who observe these patterns may be discouraged and disengage, sensing that their input carries little real impact. Educators must learn that the knowledge and input that parents provide can be critically important in making meaningful and informed educational decisions.

Another problem arises when professionals expect parents to be advocates for their children, but the parents do not behave as advocates because they view the professionals as experts. Nonmainstream parents may be particularly disinclined to challenge professional judgments. In these cases, parents may withdraw from participation but still appear to defer to professionals (Harry, 1992). In other cases, nonmainstream parents frequently find that they are "unable to advocate effectively for the needs of their children and are too often regarded as incapable of participating effectively or as unwilling to do so" (Greenbaum, Martinez, & Baber, 1997, p. 180).

This state of affairs is not inevitable. Nonmainstream families have affirmative skills and experiences that are as valuable to their children's education as those in dominant culture families. In writing about low-income and low-literate homes, Darling and Paull (1994) noted that these homes "have strengths, real assets that keep hope alive. Parents…have learned survival skills—emotional, social, financial, and literacy skills" (p. 277).

WAYS TO INCREASE SCHOOL EQUITY

Most writers point to the first step in achieving respect for diversity as being self-knowledge on the part of educators themselves, a willingness to openly and critically examine one's own culture, group identities, attitudes, and values (e.g., Spindler & Spindler, 1994). As noted by Wilson (1994, p. 244), "teachers and counselors must understand their own backgrounds, their cultural ties, their traditions, and the significance of their experiences to see their culturally diverse students through caring and unbiased eyes." The second step is to examine the stereotypes held about other groups. "The most debilitating aspect of interactions between teachers and children," noted Greenbaum et al. (1997, p. 173), "arises from negative preconceived ideas about limits on achievement." This position is echoed by others. Fritzberg (2001), for example, cautioned that such ideas are responsible for teachers and administrators interacting with nonmainstream children differently than with dominant culture children.

Educators need to know about the link established by research between stereotype threat and student underperformance (Okagaki, 2001). And they need to also understand how school practices based on stereotypes function to reproduce the economic status quo by "channeling different groups into different economic slots" (Greenbaum et al., 1997, p. 174), and "preserving the interests of the privileged" (Calabrese, 1990, p. 153). Privilege is maintained by continuation of an "us" versus "them" dichotomy, in which positive traits are attributed to the former and negative ones to the latter.

Family members and their children should be encouraged to serve as "key sociocultural informants" (Rodriguez et al., 1997, p. 135). The sharing of information about backgrounds, experiences, hopes, and aspirations can serve to enlarge and transform our traditional images of family life. To strengthen the connections between diverse kinds of families and schools, the knowledge families can impart needs to be sought out, respected, welcomed, shared, and built into curriculums (Thompson, Mixon, & Serpell, 1996).

ROLE OF SCHOOL CONSULTANTS

Consultants can work within school systems to achieve equity for nonmainstream parents so that they may have a voice equal to that of middle-class White parents. We see this work as involving consultation with teachers, school administrators, and both formal and informal parent groups. All consultation should be routinely done within "a framework that addresses cultural diversity" (Ingraham, 2000, p. 323). And, serious striving for equity in the schools requires that all school professionals bring their work to bear on challenging the many forms of oppression faced by nonmainstream families (Swadener & Lubeck, 1995). School counselors are being urged "to be agents of change" and leaders in collaboration between schools and communities "to remove institutional and environmental barriers to learning and achieving" (Stone & Hanson, 2002, pp. 188–189). There should be the same expectations for all who provide consultation—school psychologists, social workers, community psychologists, and others (Zins, Elias, Greenberg, & Pruett, 2000).

Consultants can bring to this work their skills as communicators, their knowledge of relevant theoretical and empirical literature, and their commitment to helping schools become more effective by providing environments for learning in which diversity in ethnicity, social class, and family background is valued. Consultants can suggest strategies that go beyond verbal assurances and that involve real changes in schools and the behaviors of teachers and administrators so that the participation of nonmainstream parents will be encouraged and facilitated. For example, inservice training for teachers can be modeled after such preservice courses as one described by Blasi (2002) that was effective in changing views to a "family first perspective" in which nonmainstream children and families were viewed as being "'of promise' rather than 'at risk'" (p. 106). Other programs for sensitizing teachers to multicultural issues have been well described (e.g., Milner, 2003).

Consultants can also work directly with nonmainstream parents to help them appreciate the resources they can bring to the schools and assist them in the development of additional resources. Successful strategies have been described in the literature for organizing and maintaining school-based parent support and empowerment groups (e.g., Simoni & Adelman, 1993; see also Lott, 2003). These strategies have elements in common such as building relationships with parents that begin with where the parents are, tapping into parent experiences and knowledge, encouraging dialogue and mutual respect and trust, offering options for family involvement, and connecting families with resources in the community (Ho, 2002; Lewis & Forman, 2002). Children from nonmainstream families need to see that their teachers and other school personnel respect their parents and acknowledge that they can play a crucial role in their children's education (Slaughter-Defoe, 1997).

ARTICLES IN THIS SPECIAL ISSUE

The articles in this issue illustrate the general statements in our introduction by discussing and citing examples of empirical research—quantitative or qualitative—that represent intervention efforts in the interest of increasing equity in our schools. Each article references, reviews, and critiques literature that is relevant to the work of school consultants, either because of a direct focus on consultation strategies or because of an in-depth attention to an area of stark inequity in our schools. In addition, each suggests a research agenda within the specific area of inquiry. What follows is a brief description of each article and an indication of its unique contribution.

Jeltova and Fish (this issue) address the current state of relationships between traditional schools and nonheterosexual parents. They argue for the need for systemic change for schools to provide friendly and respectful environments for gay, lesbian, and transgender (GLBT) parents and their children. Such environments must not only be free from harassment and discrimination but must also welcome the contributions of these families. The authors describe GLBT families as diverse, examine the barriers to serving their needs, and offer valuable suggestions for how school consultants can constructively and effectively intervene to transform schools so that they are "GLBT-friendly."

An in-depth case study of a participatory action research project involving youth from one neighborhood in the South Bronx of New York City is the subject of the contribution by Guishard, Fine, Doyle, Jackson, Staten, and Webb (this issue). Although the first two authors are psychologists, the latter four are teenagers who took part in the project. The authors describe their low-income, largely Latino and African American community as one that is poor in material goods but rich in resilience and explain their determination to raise consciousness about the serious and insidious "educational opportunity gap" that affects the community's families. In an effort to understand the roots and consequences of this gap in achievement and opportunity, the project used archival data, focus groups, interviews, and oral histories obtained from a parent group "Mothers on the Move/Madres en Movimiento (MOM)." This group, in existence since 1994, had organized to effect social justice changes in participants' local schools. The project described here sought to explore perceptions of educational resources, opportunities, and aspirations, and, in so doing, to awaken "critical consciousness" of the community's circumstances and action potentials.

Koonce and Harper (this issue) focus on school equity issues faced by African American parents in an urban community. They are specifically concerned with the problems these parents, who are also of low income, often have in being effective participants in school-parent dialogues and in being successful advocates for their children. They describe a model for consultation that involves cooperation with community service organizations to which the families have gone for assistance. Consultation involves the families, community organizations, psychological consultants, and school personnel.

Ochoa and Rhodes (this issue) discuss concrete steps that consultants can take to help bilingual parents achieve equity in the schools. These authors present important demographic data on bilingual children and review the different programs currently in use that assist such children. They also summarize findings from research about the relative effectiveness of the programs. The authors stress the importance and difficulties of applying the knowledge about bilingual issues to practice in school settings.

We also pay attention to the special circumstances of consultation with migrant families. Clare, Jimenez, and McClendon (this issue) write with deep respect about such families as they consider issues of family life, culture, language, and the challenges of migrant labor. Readers are led to an appreciation of what migrant Mexican families can contribute to the education of their children, and consultants are urged to shift from a deficit perspective to an asset perspective when interacting with these families.

This special issue ends with a contribution by Bonnie Nastasi (this issue) that integrates the individual articles, summarizes their insights, and draws the reader's attention to their common features. Tentative conclusions are drawn that, hopefully, will assist school consultants in their role as change agents for equity.

SUMMARY AND CONCLUSIONS

The most significant role that school consultants can play as change agents for equity is to assist parents in bringing their voices into discussions about the education of their children and to encourage school personnel to welcome these voices (Whitehouse & Colvin, 2001). To make sure that voices from nonmainstream parents are heard, understood, respected, and effective is a challenging objective for consultants.

Much has been written about the need for a school culture that is inclusive. Inclusive schools are not just nonhostile for minorities but are ones that appreciate that diversity expands the range of available knowledge about the world. As some have argued, such a school culture is a "moral imperative" (e.g., Friend, 1998, p. 157). Each of the articles in this issue provides an example of strategies and processes used by school professionals in advancing this imperative.

We agree with Weinstein, et al. (2004) that psychology is partly responsible "for the creation of an inequitable culture for learning [and] must assume leadership in its undoing. It must put in its place a new understanding of the malleable and diverse nature of human capability, the qualities of optimal environments that promote development, and the methods by which schools and classrooms ... can be cohearently strengthened to meet the needs of all children" (p. 518). Consultants need to function as facilitators for parents who are not accustomed to advocating for the interests of their children, feel ill-prepared and frustrated in their attempts to do so, and who have often had negative educational experiences themselves. School consultants cannot solve the social and political problems that maintain inequities in the larger communities, but they can recognize the existence of these inequities and assist schools in providing all children with truly equal access to education of the highest quality.

REFERENCES

Baron, R. M., Tom, D. Y., & Cooper, H. M. (1985). Social class, race, and teacher expectations. In J. B. Dusek (Ed.), *Teacher expectations* (pp. 245–259). Hillsdale, NJ: Lawrence Erlbaum Associates, Inc.

Blasi, M. J. W. (2002). An asset model: Preparing preservice teachers to work with children and families "of promise." *Journal of Research in Childhood Education, 17,* 106–121.

Bray, J. H., & Berger, S. H. (1992). Stepfamilies. In M. E. Procidano & C. B. Fisher (Eds.), *Contemporary families: A handbook for school professionals* (pp. 57–80). New York: Teachers College Press.

Calabrese, R. L. (1990). The public school: A source of alienation for minority parents. *Journal of Negro Education, 59,* 148–154.

Center on Juvenile & Criminal Justice. (2000, April 12). *School house hype: Two years later.* Retrieved January 22, 2004, from http://www.cjcj.org/pubs/schoolhouse/shh2.html

Christenson, S. L., Rounds, T., & Franklin, M. J. (1992). Home-school collaboration: Effects, issues, and opportunities. In S. L. Christenson & J. C. Conoley (Eds.), *Home-school collaboration: Enhancing children's academic and social competence* (pp. 19–51). Silver Spring, MD: National Association of School Psychologists.

Christenson, S. L., Sinclair, M. F., Lehr, C. A., & Godbar, Y. (2001). Promoting successful school completion: Critical conceptual and methodological guidelines. *School Psychology Quarterly, 16,* 468–484.

Cobb, D. E., & Medway, F. (1978). Determinants of effectiveness in parent consultation. *Journal of Clinical Child and Adolescent Psychology, 6,* 229–240.

Comer, J. P., & Haynes, N. M. (1992). Parent involvement in school: An ecological approach. *The Elementary School Journal, 91,* 271–278.

Darling, S., & Paull, S. (1994). Implications for family literacy programs. In D. K. Dickinson (Ed.), *Bridges to literacy: Children, families, and schools* (pp. 273–284). Cambridge, MA: Blackwell.

Delgado-Gaitan, C., & Trueba, H. (1991). *Crossing cultural borders: Education for immigrant families in America.* Oxford, England: Taylor & Francis.

Dusek, J. B., & Joseph, G. (1983). The bases of teacher expectancies: A meta-analysis. *Journal of Educational Psychology, 75,* 327–346.

Edens, J. F. (1997). Home visitation programs with ethnic minority families: Cultural issues in parent consultation. *Journal of Educational and Psychological Consultation, 8,* 373–383.

Elliott, S. N., & Sheridan, S. M. (1992). Consultation and teaming: Problem solving among educators, parents, and support personnel. *The Elementary School Journal, 92,* 315–338.

Entwistle, D. R., & Alexander, K. L. (1988). Factors affecting achievement test scores and marks of Black and White first graders. *The Elementary School Journal, 88,* 449–471.

Fine, M. (1993). Apparent involvement: Reflections on parents, power, and urban public schools. *Teachers College Record, 94,* 682–710.

Friend, R. A. (1998). Heterosexism, homophobia, and the culture of schooling. In S. Books (Ed.), *Invisible children in the society and its schools* (pp. 137–166). Mahwah, NJ: Lawrence Erlbaum Associates, Inc.

Fritzberg, G. J. (2001). Less than equal: A former urban schoolteacher examines the causes of educational disadvantagement. *Urban Review, 33,* 107–129.

Garibaldi, A. M. (1992). Educating and motivating African American males to succeed. *Journal of Negro Education, 61,* 4–11.

Gersten, J. C. (1992). Families in poverty. In M. E. Procidano & C. B. Fisher (Eds.), *Contemporary families: A handbook for school professionals* (pp. 137–158). New York: Teachers College Press.

Greenbaum, S., Martinez, Y. G., & Baber, M. Y. (1997). Culture and school-based policy issues. In J. L. Paul, N. H. Berger, P. G. Oskes, Y. G. Martinez, & W. C. Morse (Eds.), *Ethics and decision making in local schools: Inclusion, policy, and reform* (pp. 165–182). Baltimore: Brookes.

Greene, L., Kamps, D., Wyble, J., & Ellis, C. (1999). Home-based consultation for parents of young children with behavioral problems. *Child and Family Behavior Therapy, 21,* 19–45.

Harry, B. (1992). *Cultural diversity, families, and the special education system: Communication and empowerment.* New York: Teachers College Press.

Harry, B., Allen, N., & McLaughlin, M. (1995). Communication versus compliance: African–American parents' involvement in special education. *Exceptional Children, 61,* 364–377.

Heller, L. R., & Fantuzzo, J. W. (1993). Reciprocal peer tutoring and parent partnership: Does parent involvement make a difference? *School Psychology Review, 22,* 517–534.

Henderson, A. (1987). *The evidence continues to grow: Parent involvement improves student achievement.* Columbia, MD: National Committee for Citizens in Education.

Ho, B. S. (2002). Application of participatory action research to family-school intervention. *School Psychology Review, 31,* 106–121.

Ingraham, C. L. (2000). Consultation through a multicultural lens: Multicultural and cross-cultural consultation in schools. *School Psychology Review, 29,* 320–343.

Kalyanpur, M., Harry, B., & Skrtic, T. (2000). Equity and advocacy expectations of culturally diverse families' participation in special education. *International Journal of Disability, Development and Education, 47,* 119–136.

Kalyanpur, M., & Rao, S. S. (1991). Empowering low-income Black families of handicapped children. *American Journal of Orthopsychiatry, 61,* 523–532.

Kozol, J. (1991). *Savage inequalities.* New York: HarperCollins.

Lewis, A. E., & Forman, T. A. (2002). Contestation or collaboration? A comparative study of home-school relations. *Anthropology and Education Quarterly, 33,* 60–89.

Lindholm-Leary, K. (2000). *Biliteracy for a global society: An idea book on dual language education.* Washington, DC: National Clearinghouse for Bilingual Education.

Lott, B. (2001). Low-income parents and the public schools. *Journal of Social Issues, 57,* 247–260.

Lott, B. (2002). Cognitive and behavioral distancing from the poor. *American Psychologist, 57,* 100–110.

Lott, B. (2003). Recognizing and welcoming the standpoint of low-income parents in the public schools. *Journal of Educational and Psychological Consultation, 14,* 91–104.

Marcus, R. F., & Sanders-Reio, J. (2001). The influence of attachment on school completion. *School Psychology Quarterly, 16,* 427–444.

Maruyama, G. (2003). Disparities in educational opportunities and outcomes: What do we know and what can we do? *Journal of Social Issues, 59,* 653–676.

Metz, M. H. (1994). Desegregation as necessity and challenge. *Journal of Negro Education, 63,* 64–76.

Meyers, B. (2002). The contract negotiation stage of a school-based cross-cultural organizational consultation: A case study. *Journal of Educational and Psychological Consultation, 13,* 151–183.

Milner, H. R. (Ed.). (2003). Teacher reflection and race in cultural contexts [Special issue]. *Theory into Practice, 42*(3).

Morrison, G. M., & D'Incau, B. (1997). The web of zero intolerance: Characteristics of students who are recommended for expulsion from school. *Education and Treatment of Children, 20,* 316–335.

National Center for Education Statistics. (2001). *Digest of education statistics, Table 108, dropout rates in the United States.* Washington, DC: U.S. Department of Education.

National Center for Education Statistics. (2002a). *Digest of education statistics 2001.* Washington, DC: U.S. Department of Education.

National Center for Education Statistics. (2002b). *Schools and staffing survey, 1999–2000: Overview of the data for public, private, public charter, and Bureau of Indian Affairs elementary and secondary schools.* Washington, DC: U.S. Department of Education.

Nelson, D., & Rogers, M. R. (2002). Silenced voices: A case of racial and cultural intolerance in the schools. In A. Burzstyn & C. Korn (Eds.), *Case studies in cultural transition: Rethinking multicultural education* (pp. 13–29). New York: Greenwood.

Okagaki, L. (2001). Triarchic model of minority children's school achievement. *Educational Psychologist, 36,* 9–20.

Pigott, R. L., & Cowen, E. L. (2000). Teacher race, child race, racial congruence, and teacher ratings of children's school adjustment. *Journal of School Psychology, 38,* 177–196.

Procidano, M. E., & Fisher, C. B. (1992). Dual-wage families. In M. E. Procidano & C. B. Fisher (Eds.), *Contemporary families: A handbook for school professionals* (pp. 17–35). New York: Teachers College Press.

Raffaele, L. M., & Knoff, H. M. (2003). Who gets suspended from school and why: A demographic analysis of schools and disciplinary infractions in a large school district. *Education and Treatment of Children, 26,* 30–51.

Rodriguez, C. R., Taylor, E. L, Rosseli, H., & Thomas, D. (1997). Gender, schools, and caring: Feminist and womanist perspectives. In J. L. Paul, N. H. Berger, P. G. Oskes, Y. G. Martinez, & W. C. Morse (Eds.), *Ethics and decision making in local schools: Inclusion, policy, and reform* (pp. 123–147). Baltimore: Brookes.

Savin-Williams, R. C. (1994). Verbal and physical abuse as stressors in the lives of lesbian, gay male and bisexual youths: Associations with school problems, running away, substance abuse, prostitution and suicide. *Journal of Consulting and Clinical Psychology, 62,* 261–269.

Schramm, T. (1994). Players along the margin: Diversity and adaptation in a lower track classroom. In G. Spindler & L. Spindler (Eds.), *Pathways to cultural awareness: Cultural therapy with teachers and students* (pp. 61–91). Thousand Oaks, CA: Corwin Press.

Sears, J. T. (1991). Educators, homosexuality, and homosexual students: Are personal feelings related to professional beliefs? *Journal of Homosexuality, 22,* 29–79.

Sheridan, S. M. (1993). Models for working parents. In J. E. Zins, T. R. Kratochwill, & S. N. Elliott (Eds.), *Handbook of consultation services for children: Applications in educational and clinical settings* (pp. 110–133). San Francisco: Jossey-Bass.

Sheridan, S. M. (2000). Considerations of multiculturalism and diversity in behavioral consultation with parents and teachers. *School Psychology Review, 29,* 344–353.

Simoni, J. M., & Adelman, H. S. (1993). School-based mutual support groups for low-income parents. *Urban Review, 25,* 335–350.

Slaughter-Defoe, D. T. (1997). Ethnicity, poverty, and children's educability: A developmental perspective. In D. Johnson (Ed.), *Minorities and girls in school* (pp. 37–64). Thousand Oaks, CA: Sage.

Smith, E. P., Connell, C. M., Wright, G., Sizer, M., Norman, J. M., Hurley, A., et al. (1997). An ecological model of home, school, and community partnerships: Implications for research and practice. *Journal of Educational and Psychological Consultation, 8,* 339–360.

Spindler, G., & Spindler, L. (1994). What is cultural therapy? In G. Spindler & L. Spindler (Eds.), *Pathways to cultural awareness: Cultural therapy with teachers and students* (pp. 1–33). Thousand Oaks, CA: Corwin Press.

Stanard, R. P. (2003). High school graduation rates in the United States: Implications for the counseling profession. *Journal of Counseling and Development, 81,* 217–221.

Stone, C. B., & Hanson, C. (2002). Selections of school counselor candidates: Future directions at two universities. *Counselor Education & Supervision, 41,* 175–192.

Streeter, C. L., & Franklin, C. (1991). Psychological and family differences between middle class and low income dropouts: A discriminant analysis. *The High School Journal, 74,* 211–219.

Swadener, B. B., & Lubeck, S. (1995). The social construction of children and families "at risk": Introduction. In B. B. Swadener & S. Lubeck (Eds.), *Children and families "at promise": Deconstructing the discourse of risk* (pp. 1–14). Albany: State University of New York Press.

Thompson, R., Mixon, G., & Serpell, R. (1996). Engaging minority students in reading: Focus on the urban learner. In L. Baker, P. Afflerbach, & D. Reinking (Eds.), *Developing engaged readers in school and home communities* (pp. 43–63). Mahwah, NJ: Lawrence Erlbaum Associates, Inc.

Tucker, C. M., Zayco, R. A., Herman, K. C., Reinke, W. M., Trujillo, M., Carraway, K., et al. (2002). Teacher and child variables as predictors of academic engagement among low-income African American children. *Psychology in the Schools, 39,* 477–488.

United States Census. (2001). *Statistical abstract of the United States.* Washington, DC: U.S. Census Bureau.

Weinstein, R. S. (2002). Overcoming inequality in schooling. A call to action for community psychology. *American Journal of Community Psychology, 30,* 21–42.

Weinstein, R. S., Gregory, A., & Strambler, M. J. (2004). Intractable self-fulfilling prophecies: Fifty years after Brown v. Board of Education. *American Psychologist, 59,* 511–520.

Wentzel, K. R. (1994). Relations of social goal pursuit to social acceptance, classroom behavior, and perceived social support. *Journal of Educational Psychology, 86,* 173–182.

Whitehouse, M., & Colvin, C. (2001). "Reading" families: Deficit discourse and family literacy. *Theory into Practice, 40,* 212–219.

Wilson, P. (1994). Working on cultural issues with students: A counseling psychologist's perspective. In G. Spindler & L. Spindler (Eds.), *Pathways to cultural awareness: Cultural therapy with teachers and students* (pp. 221–245). Thousand Oaks, CA: Corwin Press.

Zimmerman, R. S., Khoury, E. L., Vega, W. A., Gil, A. G., & Warheit, G. J. (1995). Teacher and parent perceptions of behavior problems among a sample of African American, Hispanic, and non-Hispanic White students. *American Journal of Community Psychology, 23*, 181–197.

Zins, J. E., Elias, M. J., Greenberg, M. T., & Pruett, M. K. (Eds.). (2000). Implementation of prevention programs [Special issue]. *Journal of Educational and Psychological Consultation, 11*(1).

Bernice Lott is Professor Emerita of Psychology and Women's Studies at the University of Rhode Island and the author of numerous theoretical and empirical articles, chapters, and books in the areas of social learning, gender, poverty, and other social issues. Her areas of interest are interpersonal discrimination; the intersections among gender, ethnicity, and social class; the social psychology of poverty; and multicultural issues. Currently, she represents Division 9 (SPSSI) on the Council of Representatives of the American Psychological Association.

Margaret R. Rogers is an Associate Professor in the Psychology Department at the University of Rhode Island. Her research interests include school-based consultation, multicultural training in psychology, and cross-cultural competencies of school psychologists.

JOURNAL OF EDUCATIONAL AND PSYCHOLOGICAL CONSULTATION, *16*(1&2), 17–33

Creating School Environments Responsive to Gay, Lesbian, Bisexual, and Transgender Families: Traditional and Systemic Approaches for Consultation

Ida Jeltova

Fairleigh Dickinson University

Marian C. Fish

Queens College, City University of New York

The authors review research on (a) gay, lesbian, bisexual, and transgender (GLBT) families and the nature of discrimination against them; (b) school factors that hinder and facilitate equity for GLBT families; (c) instituting change through organizational consultation or large group-level strategies; and (d) instituting change through traditional consultation or small group and individual level strategies. Taking an ecological perspective, the school is viewed as a system trying to maintain the status quo in the face of increasing pressures to change. The need for systemic change when establishing antiharassment and GLBT-friendly environments in schools is highlighted. The consultant identifies the obstacles hindering change and empowers the system to reorganize itself and connect with resources that will help establish collaboration between straight and gay members of the school community. This role requires a unique combination of expertise in social processes, group dynamics, organizational change, and GLBT issues. Specific consultant strategies for small groups and individuals are identified. Resources for consultants and future research directions also are provided.

Correspondence should be sent to Ida Jeltova, 1000 River Rd., Fairleigh Dickinson University, Teaneck, NJ 07666. E-mail: jeltova@fdu.edu

The once idealized "modern nuclear family" is no longer the norm in the United States (Johnson & O'Connor, 2002; Walsh, 2003). There is now acknowledgement that parents may be biological, adoptive, step, or foster, that they may be single or in a couple, and that they may be married, divorced, widowed, remarried, or in a partnership, gay, straight, or transgender. Yet, social institutions, including schools, are often steeped in the more traditional family model, and despite efforts to adapt to the needs of changing and diverse family structures, they often lag behind societal realities.

A well-established literature demonstrates that parent-school partnerships benefit all students (e.g., Esler, Godber, & Christenson, 2002), and school consultants have been called on to move schools forward in developing school environments that allow for the full participation of all parents as cocontributors to their children's education. Over the last few decades, the changing family demographics have led to efforts to collaborate with families with diverse structures, including single-parent and stepfamilies (e.g., Bozett, 1987; Carlson, 1995; Schwartz, 1999).

In recent years, people who are gay have received increased attention in the media. Almost daily there is a newspaper or a TV program inviting examination of gay marriage, gay parenting, gays in the Army, schools for gay students, or gays in the entertainment industry. In addition, more sexual minority families are identifying themselves in the schools (Patterson, 2003; Ryan & Martin, 2000). This attention has resulted in increased visibility for gay, lesbian, bisexual, and transgender (GLBT) families and necessitates reconsideration of their relationships with schools (Ryan & Martin, 2000).

The goal of this article is to discuss how school consultants can help create school environments that are responsive to GLBT families. It describes (a) GLBT families and the nature of discrimination against them, (b) school factors that hinder and facilitate equity for GLBT families, (c) instituting change through organizational consultation or large group level strategies, (d) instituting change through traditional consultation via small group and individual level strategies, (e) directions for future research, and (f) resources for consultants. This article distinguishes between traditional and systemic approaches for consultation in schools. Traditional consultation models are the most frequently used consultative models in schools (e.g., instructional, behavioral, and mental health). These models often assume that there is a single source for a problem (e.g., instructional, mental health) and rely on indirect delivery of small group and individual interventions. Systemic consultative methods are emerging as highly effective, assume that problems result from interactions of multiple sources, and employ both small group-individual and large group-organizational interventions. Taking an ecological perspective, the consultant can focus on empowering all parties involved and establishing collaboration between straight and gay members of the school community.

GLBT FAMILIES: SEXUAL DIVERSITY IN PARENTING AND FAMILIES

Sexual orientation is defined by a person's emotional and physical attraction to other people (of their own sex, the opposite sex, or both sexes). Homosexuality refers to sexual orientation where an individual is attracted to individuals of the same sex. Gay is used to describe a man who is attracted to other men, and lesbian is used to describe a woman who is attracted to other women. Heterosexuality refers to sexual orientation where an individual is attracted to individuals of the other sex (these individuals are labeled as straight). Finally, individuals who are attracted to both sexes are described as bisexual. Although sexual orientation refers to one's behavior, sexual identity refers to one's internal definition and expression of one's sex, which may be different from one's physical sex. Transgender refers to someone whose sexual identity, including one's internal definition and expression of one's sex, may be different from his or her physical sex (Parents, Families and Friends of Lesbians and Gays [PFLAG], 2003; Ponton, 2003). Distinctions can be made between "closeted," "out," and "partially out" individuals. People who choose not to disclose their sexual orientation or identity are often referred to as "closeted." People who disclose their sexual orientation to a selected group of people (e.g., family, close circle of friends) but not others (e.g., coworkers) are said to be partially out of the closet or "partially out." Individuals who are open about their sexual orientation across all spheres of their lives are referred to as "out." Families of individuals who are gay, lesbian, bisexual, or transgender are often referred to as "gay families" and can also be described as "out," "closeted," or "partially out" (Lamme & Lamme, 2002).

It is estimated that there are as many as 5 million lesbian mothers and 3 million gay fathers in the United States (Patterson, 1992) with between 6 and 14 million children with GLBT parents (Ryan & Martin, 2000). The numbers are not precise, as many individuals do not disclose their way of life for fear of discrimination against them and their children. This fear is realistic and studies show that there is continuing discrimination against GLBT people in the United States (Gay, Lesbian, and Straight Education Network [GLSEN], 2001; Laird, 1993). GLBT individuals face discrimination that is compounded by the fact that some are immigrants, minority, poor, and so forth. Discrimination can occur through active (e.g., verbal or physical assault) or passive (e.g., lack of discrimination laws) means, and at multiple levels (e.g., classroom rules, state policies).

The majority of empirical studies on GLBT issues in school communities concern themselves with the GLBT students and not with the GLBT parents. A review of multiple sources (e.g., books, Web sites) and informal interviews with gay and lesbian parents (e.g., informal interviews in person and online), as well as activists for GLBT rights in school, suggest that experiences of GLBT parents in school are often similar to that of GLBT students and are affected by the school environment, seen as gay hostile or gay friendly (e.g., Kozik-Rosabal, 2000; Lamme & Lamme, 2002; Woog, 1995).

There is evidence describing what makes GLBT student experiences in schools negative and what contributes to positive experiences. In 2001, the GLSEN conducted the National School Climate Survey involving 904 students from 48 different states and the District of Columbia. Results revealed that 83.2% of GLBT students experienced homophobic remarks from their peers, 65% reported being sexually harassed, 40% reported being harassed physically, and 21% reported physical assault. The lack of corrective action from the school staff was cited as a contributing factor to GLBT students' feeling unsafe in schools (GLSEN, 2001). The Hostile Hallways Survey found that schools often ignore the harassment that takes place in school buildings, whether it is bullying or sexual harassment (American Association of University Women Educational Foundation, 2001). In the case of homophobia, many schools fail to acknowledge the problem and consequently fail to have any supportive resources available for the students (GLSEN, 2001). The impact on GLBT students is traumatic; they feel unsafe and gradually come to disassociate from the school community and drop out of school (e.g., 30% of GLBT students had skipped classes because they felt unsafe in the classroom; GLSEN, 2001). The percentage of GLBT students who were more likely to feel safer and have a sense of belonging in the school community was 38.1% when the schools provided positive portrayals of gay people, 35.1% when the school had a staff member supportive of GLBT students, and 62.9 % when the school had gay–straight alliances or another type of club that addressed GLBT issues (GLSEN, 2001).

Although this research looks at GLBT students, it only suggests the problems that GLBT families face. Discrimination against children who have GLBT parents may take different forms, and the children's coping responses may be different as well. Research indicates that any kind of harassment and discrimination in the school community destabilizes the learning environment by engendering fear and causing division among members of the school community (Roberts & Coursol, 1996). The establishment of a safe atmosphere in schools requires a shift in collective thinking and involves systemic change.

SCHOOL FACTORS THAT HINDER AND FACILITATE EQUITY FOR GLBT FAMILIES

School systems have always reflected the larger society as they complied with and perpetuated ideological and political imperatives of the group in power (Perkinson, 1995). Systems strive to maintain the status quo. It is only in recent years that American schools have begun addressing the issues of diversity and multiculturalism, including sexual diversity. The school system's resistance to recognizing and accepting diversity is understandable as schools are facing an extremely complex task and need to be supported and empowered to overcome the pressures to maintain the status quo.

There are a number of long-standing barriers in serving GLBT families. Common obstacles originate on the societal level (global systemic obstacles) and then filter down to individual schools. Global societal obstacles include homophobia, prejudice, and societal taboos about discussing sexuality. These provide fertile ground for multiple obstacles in specific contexts of a given school system. Commonly encountered manifestations of homophobia, prejudice, and taboos on sexuality include stereotypical views of GLBT families, myths about GLBT individuals, poor communication between the schools and families on issues pertinent to the child, and avoidance or even prohibition of discussions of sexuality and diversity in sexual expression within and outside of curricula.

Often schools have had stereotypical views of GLBT families and their needs (Ryan & Martin, 2000). GLBT families are diverse, their needs are not limited to coping with discrimination related to sexual orientation, and they change as the children grow older. Families who adopt young children may be more concerned with addressing the issue of adoption with their children and providing them with a loving and supportive environment than with coming out to the children's school (James, 2002). Other important issues may be inadvertently ignored as the issues related to sexual orientation overwhelm school professionals.

Views of GLBT families are related to stereotypes about the GLBT community. Often people expect to be able to immediately recognize GLBT parents because of mannerisms, attire, and so forth (Malone & Cleary, 2002). In part, these stereotypes are supported by the bias that homosexuality makes the person different from others in all respects and that this difference is obvious. On the other hand, many GLBT parents do not actively "come out" to their children's schools because they believe that their children will then be discriminated against (Lamme & Lamme, 2002). There are agencies that can provide help to GLBT parents with establishing communication with their schools (see *Resources for Consultants* at the end of this article).

Just as in the larger society, an abundance of myths and lack of information fuels homophobia in schools. Examples include the following: "Children brought up in gay or lesbian families become gay or lesbian because they do not have appropriate role models" or "Many gay men molest young boys." Contemporary research refutes these myths (e.g., Clarke, 2001; Patterson, 2003), yet the general public is not educated about these results.

Most curricula do not deal with diverse family structures. Although a major mission of schools is to educate and empower with knowledge by providing accurate information, heterosexual bias remains strong. Heterosexuality is viewed as a norm and is implied about every individual. Because it is so ingrained, the discussion of heterosexual relationships is not as strongly associated with divulging sexual information as it is in the case of homosexual or bisexual sexual orientation. On the other hand, in general, knowledge about human sexuality and gender development is lacking in the curriculum. Consequently, some schools do not want to include topics on alternative families in their curriculums. Perhaps this is because schools are unclear as to how to include it in the curriculum. In essence, the focus should be on discussing different types of family constellations rather than on sexual behaviors of family members (Clarke, 2001; Macgillivray, 2000; Ponton, 2003; Ryan & Martin, 2000).

Schools and families often fail to establish effective communication, and as a result, each side is driven by its preconceived notions and assumptions about each other (e.g., Christenson & Sheridan, 2001; Davies, 1997; Gettinger & Guetschow, 1998). It is important that all the professionals involved in the child's school life have a meeting with the parents and develop a plan on how to deal with various questions other parents or children may have, how the parents want the staff to address them, and so forth. In one case, the school nurse called the child's home when the child had an upset stomach and refused to speak to the father. The father called the second father and the nurse said "I already spoke to Andy's dad. I need to speak to the mom. You know, moms know this stuff better. No offense.

Mr. *X.* is Andy's father ... And who are you to Andy?" (Informal interview on September 12, 2003, with a gay family).

The effort for changing the school climate needs to be initiated from both the school and the GLBT families. Although schools are reflecting beliefs and practices of a larger society, it does not mean that a given school cannot change its own beliefs and practices. On the contrary, schools have multiple strengths that make them perfect candidates for change. In particular, they work with young people who are still developing their attitudes and practices. Therefore, schools have potential for change as long as they empower the students and families.

Creating a microclimate within a given school that is different from the climate in an overall community requires systemic change. An individual or a team of individuals who will coordinate the efforts for establishing a new ecology in the school will have to perform multiple roles (e.g., educators, problem solvers). Consultants will need to work at the large group level (organizational, ecological level) and small group and individual level (psychological, behavioral level) and will utilize their expertise in social psychology, systems theory, organizational change, collaborative planning, problem solving, reframing, and habits reversal to encourage change (Curtis & Stollar, 2002).

INSTITUTING CHANGE THROUGH ORGANIZATIONAL CONSULTATION: LARGE GROUP STRATEGIES

Establishing equality for all families represents a serious challenge to the schools because it requires organizational change and strategic planning involving families, the community, and the schools. Schools rely on consultants' expertise in strategic planning, organizational change, and collaboration to facilitate changes within buildings and the community (Curtis & Stollar, 2002; Illback, Zins, & Maher, 1999; Knoff, 2002). Consultants' expertise and skills required for instituting organizational change for building equality for all families are no different from skills required for creating antibullying programs and establishing safe environments for all children.

Successful consultation will in part depend on the consultant's understanding of how the system operates. Schools are complex living organisms with established patterns of communication, problem solving, and power distribution. Also, it is staff members, families, as well as the communities, that make up the school systems. Accurate evaluations of social processes and group dynamics within each school are part of consultation and have an impact on the consultant's effectiveness. Each building has formal and informal social structures that play various roles in the system. The role of a consultant is to utilize the existing structures to initiate change within the system and help the system self-sustain change. For example, it is up to the consultant to realize who is holding the power in a specific building, who makes the decisions, implements the decisions, and sabotages the good initiatives. Havelock and Zlototow (1995) presented a model for conducting systemic consultation where they described processes for consultants to follow.

The critical component of successful consultation will be involvement of all the parties, including those appearing to hold power within the system, who may or may not be the school administrators. In some cases, informal power holders are the most senior members of the staff or the most articulate and active parents. These individuals often hold the keys to the climate in the school building. Their leverage needs to be recruited by the consultant to establish group process that is change welcoming. It may be productive to prepare the ground for consultation by gathering the power holders and decision makers together and helping them to develop a vision of what their school will look like if it is to become more inclusive and welcoming of diverse students and their families. Framing the agenda for this meeting will depend on the specific characteristics of the school, but the ultimate goals of this meeting include the following: (a) establishing an executive subsystem within the school that holds true power and is capable of making decisions that get implemented, (b) communicating to the school community that the issue of discrimination against GLBT families is taken seriously and changes are needed, and (c) learning about forces that may facilitate or resist changes from happening by meeting these forces in person.

Resistance toward systemic changes is not an abstract force, but resides within people and is maintained by those in power. To overcome the resistance, the consultant needs to become very knowledgeable about its content and holders. Overcoming resistance does not mean opposing it. It means working with resistance through reframing and restructuring individuals' thoughts and beliefs. The refutation will include working through the misconceptions and misunderstandings about GLBT issues, dispelling the myths about GLBT individuals and their families, repairing communication between all the parties in this school's system, and providing the school community with resources for initiating and maintaining change (e.g., connect them with GLBT centers that conduct training, advocate for the families, etc.).

The meeting of the executive subsystem needs to be followed by a school-wide meeting where the agenda of creating a welcoming school environment for GLBT families is introduced and everyone is invited to provide input. It may be beneficial for the members of the executive subsystem to work with small groups within the school community on what needs to be done in their school, what can be done, how it will be evident, and who would like to do it. The consultant can assist by preparing information about negative consequences of harassment and positive consequences of having a gay-friendly environment. Role-play scenarios will provide school professionals with an outlet to vent their frustration and to practice formulating reactions to harassment. For example, individuals can role-play a social exchange between three young men. One man shares that he cries when he watches melodrama. Another man says the following: "Are you gay or something? This is so gay." The third man needs to say something to address the harassing nature of the remark (PFLAG, 2003).

The vital part of introducing change in how individuals think about and react to homosexuality is providing them with alternative beliefs and behaviors. The perpetrators, the victims, and the bystanders are the three major groups that are involved in discriminatory practices. Bullying and harassment tend to occur when it is possible to compensate for one's low confidence by belittling others. The low confidence in agents of harassment is facilitated by the low level of confidence in bystanders. The bystanders need to be trained to recognize, intervene, and prevent harassment. The perpetrators need to be trained to increase their competence via means other than harassment (e.g., Banyard, Plante, & Moynihan, 2004; Hazler, 1996; Levine, Cassidy, Brazier, & Reicher, 2002).

In cases such as antigay harassment prevention, it may not always be possible to quickly initiate a real change in a way certain individuals think about GLBT families, but it is certainly possible to initiate a change in how they act by instituting a different set of responses and consequences to their discriminatory actions. For example, the staff members who may not be very clear about what constitutes antigay harassment and who, therefore, may tolerate antigay behaviors in their students and colleagues will feel that they have a firm ground for objecting to these actions once they are educated and trained on how to respond to discriminatory behaviors. The major vehicle for empowering the school professionals, the parents, and the students is educating them on such issues as the following: (a) What does it mean to be gay? (b) How does one collaborate and communicate with diverse families, including GLBT families? (c) How does one address his or her discomfort, lack of competence, or lack of experience when working with a GLBT family? (d) How does one advocate for the families? (e) How does one react when he or she witnesses harassment? (f) How often does harassment happen? (g) What forms does harassment take? (h) How are people affected by harassment? (i) What are the educational, social, and psychological consequences of experiencing harassment? Consultants can initiate and then facilitate various task forces that will be designated to develop school policies on harassment, hate, and violence against any group at school (Tolerance.org, 2004).

It is also important to understand the patterns of communication and dissemination of information within the school building (Havelock & Zlotolow, 1995). Maladaptive communication patterns are often at the root of failed efforts to change. For example, parents are often informed about important changes that are about to take place in their child's school via letters sent home with children. This route of relating the information to the parents allows for (a) parents not getting the information because the child forgets about the letter or the parent ignores "another paper from school," or (b) misinterpretation of the planned changes as parents are excluded from the discussion of the change process; they are just being informed about it. To avoid these difficulties, the consultant needs to establish communication patterns so that the information is shared, trusted, and accepted by all members of the school community.

INSTITUTING CHANGE THROUGH TRADITIONAL CONSULTATION: SPECIFIC CONSULTANT INTERVENTIONS VIA THE SMALL GROUP AND INDIVIDUAL LEVEL

A framework is provided in this article to achieve systemic changes by using specific intervention strategies. These strategies have as their goal physical and psychological changes in the school. Specific strategies are grouped by the outcomes that GLBT parents are looking for in a school: (a) acknowledgement of GLBT community and welcoming atmosphere, (b) the school's proactive stance on the issue of discrimination against GLBT families, (c) open communication about GLBT issues, (d) straight–gay alliances within the school, and (e) the implementation of a *Safe Zone* program (GLSEN, 2001; T. Bogus, personal communication, September 15, 2003; informal interviews with GLBT parents).

Acknowledgement of GLBT Community and Welcoming Atmosphere

One of the most important strategies is arranging the physical environment in a way that signals that diversity is welcomed and promoted. To clearly designate the school's stance toward sexual diversity, start with positive highlights such as books about, photographs of, and portraits of famous members of the GLBT community, rainbow flags, and continue with such preventive measures as posted school policy explicitly specifying gender harassment as an offense, and flyers with facts about discrimination and its consequences. These symbols will help to shape behavior in a positive way and communicate expectations regarding desired behavior in the school.

The School's Stance on Discrimination Against GLBT Families

A school that takes a proactive stance in preventing harassment and intervening when discrimination occurs is perceived as a welcoming and supportive environment for GLBT families. Schools may provide mandatory training for teachers, counselors, librarians, nurses, and Title IX coordinators about sexual orientation, gender identification, and anti-GLBT bullying interventions. On a more concrete level, parents want to be reassured by hearing examples of how incidents were handled. For example, one mother learned that her son was going to be sexually humiliated in a locker room. She went and spoke to the assistant principal and the teacher. The identified bullies were called in and asked to explain their intentions. The school's rules were explained to them and the consequences of their intent were clearly delineated (i.e., a police report would be filed). The parents of the identified bullies were informed of the incident and asked to come in to school and meet with the counselor and teacher (GLBT community members, personal communication, September 12, 2003; Kozik-Rosabal, 2000). This example illustrates the importance of explicitly stating and strongly enforcing zero tolerance antidiscriminatory policies (Kozik-Rosabal, 2000; informal interviews with GLBT community members, September 12, 2003).

Open Communication

Inclusive language, both verbal and printed, facilitates change in the school climate by providing individuals with accurate ways of articulating their thoughts, questions, and requests. For example, school registration forms need to allow for alternative family constellations. The letters that go out to families from schools should address *families* and children's *guardians.* These terms are far more inclusive than *parents* (e.g., Lamme & Lamme, 2002). When talking to students about families, do not limit families to heterosexual families.

A school that addresses and includes GLBT issues in both the extracurricular activities and in the curriculum in history, art history, or social sciences is a desirable environment for GLBT families (PFLAG, 2003). When covering biographies of famous writers, acknowledging the sexual orientation of Oscar Wilde and others may be one example at the high school level. Alternatively, when talking to elementary school children about their plans for the future, include books about gay and lesbian families. Parents want the schools to validate their children's reality that they are coming from loving families where parents want them to do well in class. When schools ignore or exclude GLBT issues from the curriculum, they often challenge a child's experience and prompt him or her to think that it is atypical, that it is not normal (Clarke, 2001; GLSEN, 2001; PFLAG, 2003).

Gay–Straight Alliances

Forming alliances between GLBT students and families and straight students and families has been shown to be successful in stopping and preventing harassment and in establishing a welcoming environment in the school (GLSEN, 2001; PFLAG, 2003). It is important that the school has alliances of straight and GLBT individuals because "coming out" of the closet is a two-way street. When parents see flyers and bulletin boards on gay–straight alliances they see that the school is trying to be aware, open, proactive, and supportive (T. Bogus[1], personal communication, September 15, 2003; PFLAG, 2003).

At the high school level, alliances are often run by the students with the supervision of a designated staff member trained in GLBT issues. The groups meet after classes in a space provided by the school. These meetings often provide opportunities for discussing sexual identity and gender issues with information provided to the students in an age-appropriate manner (e.g., how to talk to your parents, where to look for more support and guidance, etc.; PFLAG, 2003; T. Bogus, personal communication, September 15, 2003).

From Safe Person to Safe Zone to Safe School

Consultants can facilitate the implementation of a *Safe Person* or *Safe Zone* program (PFLAG, 2003). Under the *Safe Person* program, a designated safe person in the school system serves as a representative of the school to the

---

[1]Terry Bogus is a Director of the Gay Center in Greenvich Village, New York.

GLBT community. This person serves as a mediator who can coordinate and problem solve effectively to maintain open communication between different groups within the school. The *Safe Zone* gets established by the teacher, counselor, nurse, or any school professional joining the gay–straight alliance in the school and making his or her room or office inclusive and welcoming to GLBT individuals. The school representatives may use a separate space in their rooms where they display materials on diversity, antiharassment policies, GLBT resources, GLBT-inclusive books and videos, and health and referral information (PFLAG, 2003). Practice suggests that once several persons participate in the *Safe Zone* program, others will follow given the positive consequences of the program. GLSEN reports that positive changes occur within the first few weeks and then spread throughout the schools within a few months so that the *Safe Zone* may set off a self-perpetuating change in the school system (PFLAG, 2003; Guthrie, 1996).

DIRECTIONS FOR FUTURE RESEARCH

The success of school-wide reforms aimed at creating GLBT family-friendly environments is not well documented. Research is needed that will provide a record of variables associated with stories of success and failures of such reforms in consultative interventions. Critical in such research is its longitudinal course and the use of statistical methods appropriate for an ecological approach to research rather than traditional linear cause-and-effect paradigms. System-wide school climate measures and classroom climate scales (e.g., Classroom Systems Observation Scale; Fish & Dane, 2000) may help to assess systemic change.

Another important line of research in consultation is investigating training models that produce the most skillful systemic consultants. The informal interviews of the GLBT parents suggest that they usually either initiated the programmatic changes themselves or brought in an external consultant. This is because school professionals often lacked expertise in GLBT issues, group dynamics, and systemic interventions, which prevented them from being more proactive in their settings. It is important to question whether providing school professionals (e.g., school psychologists, counselors) with more training and practice in group dynamics and organizational change will be associated with more preventive measures.

Also, research on pathways of social and emotional development of biological versus adopted children from GLBT families will benefit the field of consultation in terms of fine-tuning the services offered by the schools and community centers. Such research helps to answer questions many school social workers, psychologists, and counselors may confront: What constitutes parent training for GLBT families with adopted children? What are the developmental issues that these children face as they grow up? How should school-based programs for children coming from GLBT families differ across elementary, middle, and high school?

Another line of future research is investigation of rural versus suburban versus urban GLBT families and their participation in schools. With the growing use of the Internet, gay rights and gay pride organizations are able to offer informational and psychological support to many, no matter how remote their locale. Besides this virtual support, what can schools do for families that do not live in areas rich with resources for the gay community? Overall, more research is needed on experiences that GLBT families have in schools.

CONCLUSION

This article presented an overview of current knowledge in GLBT research and practice in relation to school children and their families as well as recommendations on how to conduct systemic consultation to promote GLBT-friendly environments in schools. Further research is needed to empirically validate strategies described in this article. Throughout the discussion, the need for systemic change when establishing antiharassment and GLBT-friendly environments in schools was highlighted. It is clear that the contemporary public school system is under considerable stress, and if it is stagnated, it is because the system is trying to maintain the status quo when its responsibilities are being extended and its resources are decreasing. In many cases, the consultants will walk into the situations where the "bottom" level of the system (e.g., students, parents, teachers) wants change whereas the "top" level of the system (e.g., administration at all levels) can no longer regulate the system relying on old means. The consultant's role is then to establish communication between the "top" and the "bottom" levels as to empower the system to reorganize itself and to connect it with resources that will help the change to survive. This role will require a unique combination of expertise in social processes, group dynamics, organizational change, and GLBT issues.

REFERENCES

American Association of University Women Educational Foundation. (2001). *Hostile hallways. Bullying, teasing, and sexual harassment in schools.* Washington, DC: American Association of University Women.

Banyard, V. L., Plante, E. G., & Moynihan, M. M. (2004). Bystander education: Bringing together a broader community perspective on sexual violence prevention. *Journal of Community Psychology, 32,* 61–79.

Bozett, F. W. (1987). *Gay and lesbian parents.* New York: Praeger.

Carlson, C. (1995). Working with single-parent and stepfamily systems. In A. Thomas & J. Grimes (Eds.), *Best practices in school psychology* (3rd ed., pp. 1097–1110). Washington, DC: National Association of School Psychologists.

Christenson, S. L., & Sheridan, S. M. (2001). *Schools and families: Creating essential connections for learning.* New York: Guilford.

Clarke, V. (2001). What about the children? Arguments against lesbian and gay parenting. *Women's Studies International Forum, 24,* 555–570.

Curtis, M. J., & Stollar, S. A. (2002). Best practices in system-level change. *Best practices in school psychology* (4th ed., pp. 223–235). Washington, DC: National Association of School Psychologists.

Davies, D. (1997). Crossing boundaries: How to create successful partnerships with families and communities. *Early Childhood Journal, 25,* 73–77.

Esler, A. N., Godber, Y., & Christenson, S. L. (2002). Best practices in supporting home-school collaboration. In A. Thomas & J. Grimes (Eds.), *Best practices in school psychology* (4th ed., pp. 389–412). Washington, DC: National Association of School Psychologists.

Fish, M. C., & Dane, E. (2000). Classroom Systems Observation Scale: Development of an instrument to assess classrooms using a systems perspective. *Learning Environments Research, 3,* 67–92.

Gay, Lesbian, and Straight Education Network. (2001). *The national school climate survey 2001: Lesbian, gay, bisexual, and transgender students and their experiences in schools.* New York: Author.

Gettinger, M., & Guetschow, K. W. (1998). Parental involvement in schools: Parents and teacher perceptions of role, efficacy, and opportunities. *Journal of Research and Development in Education, 32*(1), 38–52.

Guthrie, L. F. (1996). Going to scale with school-community collaborations: Expanding pilot programs district wide requires capacity building and skill development. *The School Administrator, 11,* 26–32.

Havelock, R., & Zlotolow, S. (1995). *The change agents guide* (2nd ed.). Englewood Cliffs, NJ: Educational Technology Publications.

Hazler, R. J. (1996). Breaking the cycle of violence: *Interventions for bullying and victimization.* Washington, DC: Accelerated Development.

Illback, R. J., Zins, J. E., & Maher, C. A. (1999). Program planning and evaluation: Principles, procedures, and planned change. In C. R. Reynolds & T. B. Gutkin (Eds.), *The handbook of school psychology* (3rd ed., pp. 907–932). New York: Wiley.

James, S. E. (2002). Clinical themes in gay- and lesbian-parented adoptive families. *Clinical Child Psychology and Psychiatry, 7,* 475–486.

Johnson, S. M., & O'Connor, E. (2002). *The gay baby boom: The psychology of gay parenthood.* New York: New York University Press.

Knoff, H. (2002). Best practices in facilitating school reform, organizational change, and strategic planning. In A. Thomas, & J. Grimes (Eds.), *Best practices in school psychology* (4th ed., pp. 235–253). Washington, DC: National Association of School Psychologists.

Kozik-Rosabal, G. (2000). "Well, we haven't noticed anything bad going on," said the principal. Parents speak about their gay families and schools. *Education and Urban Society, 32,* 368–389.

Laird, J. (1993). Lesbian and gay families. In F. Walsh (Ed.), *Normal family processes* (2nd ed., pp. 282–328). New York: Guilford.

Lamme, L. L., & Lamme, L. A. (2002). Welcoming children from gay and lesbian families into our schools. *Educational Leadership, 59*, 65–72.

Levine, M., Cassidy, C., Brazier, G., & Reicher, S. (2002). Self-categorization and bystander non-intervention: Two experimental studies. *Journal of Applied Social Psychology, 32*, 1452–1463.

Macgillivray, I. K. (2000). Educational equity for gay, lesbian, bisexual, transgendered, and queer/questioning children: The demands of democracy and social justice for America's schools. *Education and Urban Society, 32*, 303–323.

Malone, K., & Cleary, R. (2002). (De)Sexing the family: Theorizing the social science of lesbian families. *Feminist Theory, 3*, 271–293.

Parents, Families and Friends of Lesbians and Gays. (2003). *From our house to the schoolhouse: Families and educators partnering for safe schools.* Washington, DC: Author.

Patterson, C. J. (1992). Children of lesbian and gay parents. *Child Development, 63*, 1021–1042.

Patterson, C. J. (2003). *Lesbian and gay parenting.* Retrieved September 10, 2003, from http://www.apa.org/pi/parent.html

Perkinson, H. J. (1995). *The imperfect panacea: American faith in education.* New York: McGraw-Hill.

Ponton, L. (2003). *What does gay mean? How to talk with kids about sexual orientation and prejudice: A guide from the National Mental Health Association.* Washington, DC: National Mental Health Association.

Roberts, W. B., & Coursol, D. H. (1996). Strategies for intervention with childhood and adolescent victims of bullying, teasing, and intimidation in school settings. *Elementary School Guidance and Counseling, 30*, 204–212.

Ryan, D. & Martin, A. (2000). Lesbian, gay, bisexual, and transgender parents in the school systems. *School Psychology Review, 29*, 207–216.

Schwartz, W. (1999). *Family diversity in urban schools. ERIC/CUE Digest, 14.* Washington, DC: Office of Educational Research and Improvement.

Tolerance.org. (2004). *Responding to hate at school: A guide for teachers, counselors, and administrators.* Retrieved October 15, 2004, from http://www.tolerance.org/rthas/index.jsp

Walsh, F. (2003). *Normal family processes* (3rd ed.). New York: Guilford.

Woog, D. (1995). *School's out: The impact of gay and lesbian issues on America's schools.* Boston: Alyson.

RESOURCES FOR CONSULTANTS

Books

Havelock, R., & Zlotolow, S. (1995). *The change agents guide* (2nd ed.). Englewood Cliffs, NJ: Educational Technology Publications.

Parents, Families and Friends of Lesbians and Gays. (2003). *From our house to the schoolhouse. Families and educators partnering for safe schools.* Washington, DC: Author.

Ponton, L. (2003). *What does gay mean? How to talk with kids about sexual orientation and prejudice. A guide from National Mental Health Association.* Washington, DC: National Mental Health Association.

Audio and Video Resources

It's Elementary: Talking About Gay Issues in Schools By Women's Educational Forum: http://www.youth.org/loco/PERSONProject/Resources/Videos/elementary3.html

Our House: A Very Real Documentary About Kids of Gay and Lesbian Parents by Mima Padola. Sugar Pictures: http://www.itvs.org/ourhouse

Web Sites

APA Resolution on Gay, Lesbian, and Bisexual Issues: http://www.apa.org/pi/reslgbc.html

NASP Position Statement on Gay, Lesbian and Bisexual Youth: http://www.nasponline.org/advocacy/glb.html

National Institute of Mental Health: http://www.nmha.org/whatdoesgaymean.com

School Counselor Association. Just the Facts About Sexual Orientation: A Primer for Principals, Educators, and School Personnel:

Organizations

Children of Lesbians and Gay Everywhere (COLAGE): http://www.colage.org

Gay, Lesbian, and Straight Education Network (GLSEN): http://www.glsen.org

Parents, Families and Friends of Lesbians and Gays (PFLAG): http://www.pflag.org

Students and Gay-Straight Alliances: http://www.glsen.org/templates/student

Ida Jeltova, PhD, is an Assistant Professor of School Psychology, School of Psychology, Fairleigh Dickinson University, Teaneck, NJ. Her research interests focus on family, school, and community partnerships, psychoeducational school- and community-based interventions for diverse families and children, and risk and protective factors for HIV and AIDS in youth.

Marian C. Fish is Professor of School Psychology at Queens College of the City University of New York, and Coordinator of the School Psychology Program. Her research interests include family systems, family–school relationships, equity issues, and ecological interventions in schools.

JOURNAL OF EDUCATIONAL AND PSYCHOLOGICAL CONSULTATION, 16(1&2), 35–54

The Bronx on the Move: Participatory Consultation With Mothers and Youth

Monique Guishard, Michelle Fine, Christine Doyle,
Jeunesse Jackson, Travis Staten, and Ashley Webb
The Graduate Center, City University of New York

We introduce participatory action research as a strategy for "consultation with." We elaborate the possibilities and limits of participatory consultation as a strategy that enables sustained relations with communities of material poverty and resilience wealth. Consulting with an activist organization, and dedicated to producing a Web-based oral history, we engaged youth researchers to (a) conduct individual oral histories, archival analyses, and participant observation; (b) participate in focus groups; and (c) compile their reflections on this work. The project sought to produce documentation of the history and contemporary conditions under which poor and working class mothers, a few fathers, and youth struggle for justice and social mobility, against inequity with a strong sense of responsibility as parents, as students, and as activists in low resource schools.

Although it is customary to think about consultation to an organization, on a community, for an advocacy project, we have intentionally framed our work as "consultation with." In this article, we expand the notion of consultation, and introduce a case in which we (researchers from The Graduate Center of the City University of New York) worked in partnership with mothers and youth from an activist, community-based organization, Mothers on the Move (MOM), dedicated to educational justice in the South Bronx of New York City.

Correspondence should be sent to Monique Guishard, Department of Psychology, Social-Personality Program, The Graduate Center, City University of New York, 365 Fifth Avenue, New York, NY 10016. E-mail: mguishard@gc.cuny.edu

Our consultative relationship "with" MOM developed in anticipation of their 10th anniversary. Members of the board of directors, the former director of MOM, and Graduate Center researchers developed a plan to conduct a much needed oral history of MOM's pivotal role in instigating social change directed at closing disparities in health, housing, and most notably education in the Hunts Point section of the South Bronx. We agreed that our oral history project would serve multiple purposes. First, in the climate of intensified parental and student blame for the academic achievement gap, we would help the organization chronicle the passionate historic and contemporary struggles engaged by these grandmothers, mothers, and fathers who may be low in finances, but are high on parental involvement. We wanted to create popular and scholarly documents and a Web site to disseminate widely that struggles for social justice are fervently alive in what most would describe as a materially impoverished setting, but we recognize as a community of great resilience and social capital wealth.

Second, our oral history project would assist the organization in the crafting of an explicit youth component of MOM and this would be the beginning of our consultative partnership with youth. Last, the consultation would afford researchers from the Graduate Center an opportunity to understand in a rich contextual detail, how mothers and youth cultivate an awareness of oppressive educational practices and policies that shape their futures and struggles for justice, against educational inequity in the South Bronx of New York City. This article reflects on the process, delights, and dilemmas of consultation within these very hard and very mean times.

DOCUMENTING THE STRUGGLE:
WHAT WE LEARNED

The terms of our consultation were simple—to document the history and contemporary struggles for educational justice, as sculpted by the marches, sit-ins, and protests of MOM, over the past 13 years. We developed a youth research collective to help us gather the material and create the oral history. To begin, we had to learn much about the long path of struggle blazed by MOM and about the local and national context of disparities in educational attainment. Ms. Sojourner, a MOM member, provided some of this history:

> MOMs gave us the power, the will. In the beginning, in the very beginning they enabled the community. It's like ah social justice they didn't do the work for us like social service they empowered us with social justice so we'll be able to go out here and fight for our own children …

Twenty years after the publication of "A Nation at Risk" (United States Department of Education, 1983) and fifty years after the Brown v. Board of Education Supreme Court decision (1954), race, ethnicity, and social class still overpredict the academic opportunities available to youth in the United States (Fine, 2004, Fine, et al., 2003, 2005; United States Department of Education, National Center for Education Statistics, 2000). These inequities are popularly called "the achievement gap." Ms. Sojourner, a member of MOM, aptly described these discrepancies as "setting our children up to fail:"

> I feel that our children are set up to fail, to fail the school system because if you look at the statistics as we stand now I think I'm right now I'm I'm I'm fighting against the standardized testing because they know for a fact that only fifty percent of these children are gonna pass this test. So we know what fifty percent gonna pass and we know what percent gonna fifty percent is gonna fail it, and to me that's setting our children up for prison! I mean, you know because if they can't get educated where they gonna go? A percentage gonna go out to crime, a percentage just might wind up on public assistance, and a percentage…you know. So to me I will fight till it's equal justice for our children and that's the whole bottom line. (Interview excerpt)

With the youth researchers, we scoured the literature on "the gap," gathering more evidence of inequalities—by race, ethnicity, class, and their intersections (Guishard, Doyle, et al., 2003; Guishard, Fine, et al., 2003). In this collaborative review of academic and popular articles and documents, we attained knowledge of vast ethnic disparities in educational attainment: for every 100 kindergarteners, 49% of Asian Americans, 30% of White Americans, 16% of African Americans, and 6% of Latinos will obtain a college degree (The Education Trust, 2001). We also learned that low-income (28.3%) students are substantially less likely to be enrolled in a college preparatory track compared to medium- (48.8%) and high-income students (65.1%). The combination of finance inequities, maldistribution of qualified educators, differential access to college preparatory material, low expectations, and now high stakes testing severely limit the opportunities and outcomes available to low-income youth of color (Anyon, 1997; Bowles & Gintis, 1976; Ferguson, 1998; New York ACORN Schools Office, 2000). All of these conditions, commonly called "the school to prison track," at their worst, are found in district 8 in the South Bronx of New York City.

Much research has vividly documented the systemic and historic "savage inequalities" that characterize America's schools (Anyon, 1997; Fine, 1983, 1991; Kozol, 1991). Seldom chronicled are the vibrant, passionate,

and significant community-based struggles designed to resist and inter-
rupt the miseducation of materially underprivileged youth of color. Rarely
does research also incorporate the perspective of those persons most affected by the differential access and educational opportunities—youth and
families of color from poor and working class backgrounds (for notable exceptions, see Anand, Fine, Perkins, Surrey, & The Renaissance School
Class of 2000, 2002; Bookman & Morgan, 1988; Fine, 1991; Fine & Wong,
1995; Guishard, Doyle, et al, 2003; Guishard, Fine, et al., 2003; Hill-Collins,
1998, 2001; Lareau, 2003; Lott, 2001; Lott & Bullock, 2001; O'Connor, 1997).
Recommendations for this type of inclusion and diversity in the consultation field have been eloquently made by researchers like Clare (2002). In
this spirit, this project was created as a consultative "gift" to the organization to explicate, document, archive, and create a virtual museum of struggle, so that yesterday's and today's activists could revisit and remember,
and tomorrow's could see their path.

ENTER HUNTS POINT

When one thinks about the Bronx, perhaps the last thing that comes to mind
is insurgent educational activism. The section of the South Bronx where this
study took place in many ways fits the "criteria" for a disaster area—the
poorest congressional district in the country; thousands of families living in
poverty, dilapidated, roach and rat infested housing; hundreds of empty
lots; rampant drug abuse and prostitution; and incidences of AIDS and
syphilis higher than the state of Arkansas and 18 other states (My Neighborhood Statistics, 2003; The Brooklyn AIDS Task Force, 2003). The putrid
stench emitted from this heavily industrialized zone, home to the largest
meat and produce markets in the United States, is a combination of the die-
sel fuel left by the 11,000 trucks that deliver goods to "The Point" daily and
the conversion of the majority of New York City's sewage sludge into fertil-
izer pellets. The resulting odor produces abysmal air quality and asthma
hospitalization rates that are the highest in the country. Yet amidst this
sometimes unaesthetically pleasing setting that most of us are proud to call
home, "we" find "beauty" and hope through, among other things, insurgent parent organizing and activist youth research.

Thirteen years ago a group of students and staff gathered at the Bronx Educational Services (BES), an organization that provided adult literacy and
English as a Second Language programs. BES students were comprised of
mostly poor and working-class mothers who not only emerged from neighborhood schools in Hunts Point and Longwood lacking basic literacy skills,
but were also struggling as they watched their children in transition toward

repeating their fates. Committed to joining literacy development with student empowerment (Freire, 1970, 1973), BES instructor (and MOM cofounder[1]) Barbara Gross brought in a newspaper article that ranked New York City's public schools by student standardized reading and math score performance, with the hopes that data therein would inspire her students to ask critical questions and inspire necessary action. At first glance, student reading and math performance in District 8 was relatively high compared to other school districts citywide. Indeed, for years, the performance of students in the northern, wealthier, Whiter part of the district (in the neighborhoods of Throggs Neck and Sound View, which also have a large Black middle class) masked the abysmal academic conditions and performance of students in the southern part of the district (Hunts Point and Longwood), where more poor and working-class Blacks and Latinos live.

The article Ms. Gross brought in also presented the data by individual school and revealed that schools in Hunts Point and Longwood ranked among the lowest in the city; many were dubbed Schools Under Registration Review in jeopardy of losing accreditation for persistent failure. Although BES students (parents) knew in their hearts that neighborhood schools had failed them and were now failing their children, they were nonetheless shocked at the disaggregated data. For years administrators had blamed these mothers and their workloads for their children's failure. In this toxicity of derogation, mothers had internalized some of this blame and held their heavy workloads and sometimes lack of time responsible for their children and grandchildren's underperformance. Outraged and discouraged by the article, many of the mothers' first inclination was to meet with the children and talk to them about the importance of determination and hard work despite their circumstances, while extolling the benefits of getting a "good" education. Parents soon got their opportunity and met with a group of fourth-grade students. As an introduction, the teacher stood in front of the class and admonished her young students to "listen to these people or you'll grow up to be like your parents, on welfare."

After witnessing this harsh treatment of students firsthand, parents who once blamed their children and themselves for academic "underperformance" became outraged. Their outrage multiplied as the links between the structural injustice and the (im)possibilities of social mobility for their children and grandchildren became apparent through research on education and health disparities among Hunts Point, Sound

---

[1]Milli Boñilla and Barbara Gross both organized the idea for the Parent Organizing and Education Project with Bronx Educational Services students and this organization would later become Mothers on the Move/Madres en Movimiento in 1994 (http://www.mothersonthemove.org).

View, and Throggs Neck.[2] Following a refined understanding of roots of the gap, a desire for collective action rapidly evolved. The idea for establishing a grassroots organization for parents to redress these inequities was soon born. Mothers on the Move/Madres en Movimiento incorporated in 1994.

Since then, over a thousand community residents have participated in the struggle for social change in the South Bronx. MOM launches public accountability campaigns that have resulted in the ejection of numerous principals and school board members, the removal of a superintendent in office for over 20 years, the exposure of school board election fraud and corruption, and several meetings with New York City Department of Education officials. MOM members have fundamentally reconceptualized parent involvement in South Bronx schools. No longer relegated to bake sales and school trip chaperones, these modern day Ella Bakers (Ransby, 2003) take pride in their reputation as "royal nuisances." In response to members' needs, MOM has evolved into a multi-issue organization, organizing campaigns for environmental justice: lower asthma rates, affordable and decent housing, and truck safety to prevent industrial trucks from traversing residential streets.

Today MOM serves the South Bronx neighborhoods of Hunts Point, Longwood, Port Morris, and the eastern halves of Morrisania, Melrose, and Mott Haven and has a core leadership base of approximately 100 members, with more than 250 emerging leaders and an additional 500 followers. MOM members are reflective of the Hunts Point-Longwood community; approximately 60% are Latino or Hispanic (Dominican, Puerto Rican, Caribbean, Mexican, and Central American) and 40% are African American. Members are predominantly mothers (90%), but also some fathers (10%), and primarily low income with lots of variation, from public assistance recipients to middle-class homeowners, and from teenage mothers to grandparents (the average member age is approximately 35).

CONSULTATION WITH—METHODS OF PARTICIPATION AND DOCUMENTATION

To begin our consultation with MOM, Michelle and Monique met with members and directors of MOM and together we designed a multimethod participatory action research (PAR) project. We created an explicit commitment to a

---

[2]This research was conducted in conjunction with researchers from New York University's Institute for Education and Social Policy and other organizations prior to our participatory consultation.

consultation in which we were conducting research with and not just for an organization and with youth. We generated the following three goals:

1. Establish a community of youth researchers to study how adolescents, their mothers, and community members perceive the "achievement gap" in terms of social class, race or ethnicity, and opportunity inequities.
2. Document the history of struggles waged by MOM.
3. Create varied products for organizing and scholarly publication that includes a Web site and a set of scholarly, policy, and community-youth products that will educate and arouse public and youth understanding of existing educational inequities and possibilities for action within the public education system.

We created a participatory research design, in which youth researchers would work together with adult researchers to do the following:

1. Conduct 10 interviews of founding and current MOM members asking them about their experiences in the organization and participation in the fight to close the gap in District 8.
2. Facilitate a focus group with the youth researchers to discuss how their experiences researching MOM, and witnessing their mother's and grandmother's activism, shaped their views of educational inequity.
3. Sponsor visitation to "well resourced" schools and school districts throughout urban and suburban New York State to assess what money can buy.
4. Collect archival data including newsletters, photographs, newspaper clippings, reports, signs, and organizational activist artifacts about MOM.
5. Analyze interview and focus group transcripts and archival data, utilizing theoretical coding and participatory or group inductive analysis (Patton, 2001).

PARTICIPATORY CONSULTATION

Our consultative practices drew heavily from the writings and praxis of PAR (Chataway, 1997; Fine et. al., 2003; Martín-Baró, 1994; Reason, 1994) and research on forging partnerships between the academy and oppressed communities (Nelson, Prilleltensky, & MacGillivary, 2001). Foundational to PAR lies the recognition that inquiry is always political, knowledge is embedded in unjust social relations, and research is most powerful when produced through action and in community struggle (Fine et. al., 2003;

Kemmis & McTaggart, 2000). Within a PAR project, the experiential knowledge of oppressed groups is honored, prized, and sometimes privileged over the researcher's abstract academic knowledge; products are designed to be directly useful to participants; and collective self-inquiry and reflection are structured to provoke critical consciousness (Fals-Borda, 1979; Fals-Borda & Rahman, 1991; Reason,1994). In participatory research, the conventional boundaries separating researchers from participants are intentionally blurred.

The PAR design we utilized evolved out of work we had conducted in schools, prisons, and community-based settings (see Fine et. al., 2003). In this project, there were varying degrees of participation and collaboration. Mothers and community members consulted on the design of the overall project and solicited our help in conducting an oral history of their educational activism. "Informants" for the oral histories, they were also "clients" for the bilingual Web site produced and designed by the youth.[3] Young people were even more fully engaged as paid, participant-researchers. The requirements for participation were that young people be a child or grandchild of a MOM member, enjoy writing, be enrolled in at least high school, and be able to commit to attending research methods training sessions.[4] Seven youth applied and five were accepted.[5] The junior researchers ranged in age from 14 to 21 years.

To begin our work together, youth were trained in critical social theory: critical consciousness (e.g., Freire, 1970, 1973, 1994; Hooks, 1994; Ward, 2000; Watts & Abdul-Adil, 1999; Watts, Williams, & Jagers, in press), false consciousness (e.g., Jost, Pelham, Sheldon, & Sullivan, 2003), relative deprivation (e.g., Crosby, Pufall, Snyder, O'Conell, & Whalen,1989; Deutsch, 1974; Duncan, 1999; Grant & Brown, 1995; Gurin, Miller, & Gurin, 1980; Runciman, 1966), social reproduction (e.g., Giroux, 1983), critical race theory (Crenshaw, Sotanda, Peller, & Thomas, 1995), Black feminist epistemology (Hill-Collins, 1998, 2001), and basic social science research methods, in

---

[3]The youth researchers used archival data, pictures, and excerpts of the oral history interviews to create a template on paper of the Mothers on the Move Web site. Through an internship with the New Media Lab at the Graduate Center and in conjunction with programmer Andrea Pitanga, our research team was able to create and launch the site (http://mothersonthemove.org).

[4]We would like to acknowledge Rose-Marie Roberts, an advanced Social Personality Psychology graduate student, for her integral assistance in the early stages of this project in designing and conducting research training sessions and managing the majority of our institutional review process.

[5]A fifth student, Sati Singleton, worked on early phases of this project but ended his participation in the fall of 2001.

approximately 30 research training sessions in the summer and fall of 2002 by Graduate Center researchers. Youth research training sessions were designed with substantial input from other colleagues[6] working on youth participatory research projects, and the young researchers.

The research training sessions were designed as a democratic environment to empower youth, by expanding and building on their emerging commitments to social change through inquiry. In a typical session, the research team was introduced to a particular theory and engaged in discussion regarding its context, importance, relevance, and applicability to understanding how oppressed people come to understand the conditions and ideologies that shape their disadvantages, and how they organize to challenge their individual and collective situations. An important aspect of the theoretical training involved conversations about who are social theorists, what methods are utilized in studies, and whose voices and perspectives are privileged and silenced in social research. Sessions lasted 2 hours, and in addition to problem posing, group discussion, and practical exercises, the sessions were designed to engage the youth in a process of learning, which took seriously their experiential knowledge and their preconceived notions of research, researchers, and the researched. The youth researchers took notes, represented material back to each other and the session facilitator, and had opportunities to practice research techniques with each other.

Our junior research team members were paid $300 for their participation in the summer, received three college credits for their work in the fall, and were acknowledged as coauthors in scholarly articles when they contributed their writing and critique. Youth participation also entailed the following: devising the interview protocol used in the oral history, conducting the interviews, engaging in participant observation of educational activist events, consulting on products (articles and the Web site), writing up and presenting their research at national and local conferences, and informing analyses.

ANALYSIS

Relying on critical justice studies (scholars such as Morton Deutsch, Paolo Freire, Ignacio Martín-Baró, Patricia Hill-Collins, Michelle Fine, and Susan Opotow), we began our analyses with a set of theoretical assumptions

---

[6]The City University of New York Graduate Center research team includes Michelle Fine, Jen Ayala, Janice Bloom, April Burns, Lori Chajet, Monique Guishard, Maria Torre, Yasser Payne, Tiffany Perkins-Munn, and Kersha Smith.

about how parents and youth develop a sense of injustice of educational inequity. We were specifically interested to understand how these assumptions would play out contextually, through MOM's organizing for education reform and participatory youth inquiry.

Drawing from these disparate educational, political, and psychological theories, and taking seriously the experiences and explanations offered by the youth, we utilized what Patton (2001) described as a participatory or group inductive analysis. After the youth researchers transcribed the interviews, and analyzed the data, we collectively organized participant responses by interview questions that we felt were most relevant to understanding how mothers perceived the achievement gap, injustice in general, and their justice attributions. We coded these responses into the provisional categories, relying on moments of critical consciousness as our primary unit of analysis. We read across responses to capture emergent themes within this larger category and worked together until we established interrater reliability of at least 90% and then developed theoretical narratives. We have presented this work in scores of settings—to activists, policymakers, youth researchers, educators, research psychologists—and have been joined by what we might call "intersite" reliability in which the dynamics of critical consciousness and action, linked through critical inquiry, have been replicated as an important theoretical element of youth-based community organizing.

The youth data we present in this article derive from free writing in research training sessions, presentations, e-mail correspondence, and a research paper on the evolution of their own critical consciousness over the course of this project. The primary authors made these selections with the approval of our coresearchers. We are currently in the process (Guishard et al., 2005) of analyzing the youth researcher focus group, converting our inductive frames to conceptual maps using Atlas Ti, and working toward theoretical triangulation (Patton, 2001) by analyzing moments of critical consciousness from other theoretical perspectives. In this article, we focus largely on youth critical consciousness as evidence in the activist PAR and we selectively illustrate parallel or complementary insights from mothers in their organizing efforts.

LEARNINGS: PARTICIPATORY ACTION RESEARCH AS A STRATEGY OF CONSULTATION WITH

Through this experience I've learned so many things. I think…no I know for sure that I believe in the standpoint theory. Who I am matters. Through this project I have grown not only into a youth researcher, but an activist. A proud, youth activist. I also hope that people realize justice is not blind and changes need to be made in our social status as a whole. (Ashley, Youth Researcher, excerpt from essay on critical consciousness development)

Our consultation with youth was largely about cultivating, not developing, critical consciousness. This distinction is critical. We began from the assumption that youth and mothers in the South Bronx already know a great deal about educational oppression. Our collaboration worked toward growing a shared vocabulary for describing, theorizing, and disseminating the work. As the youth found a vocabulary for naming injustice, they stretched their individual experiences into generalizable collective experiences:

In the beginning I had no idea what the achievement gap was however, I knew there was a word to describe my harsh experiences while attending public school. I would go about my curriculum everyday of school believing that every thing was fair and believing in the American Dream. That if I try my hardest at excelling in all of my subjects and keep at it until I finished college, I too can achieve the American Dream. I would be a successful Black American man with a loving family to come home to after a long days work. I would be living in a nice neighborhood, with a dog, picket fences and the whole nine yards. My school I felt then was great because I hadn't had the experience to compare it to any other school. I never realized that I had never built any sort of relationship with my teachers. I would just go through class writing down assignments, raising my hand in class to let the teacher know that all of her students weren't actually dead, and completing to the best of my ability the homework assignments... With all of this I have learned that very few people actually do achieve the "American Dream." There is a struggle taking place in our school system and today millions and millions of children are at war. War in their household, at school and in inner-city streets. It is a shame that children are the casualties in this battle of equality. It's a tough battle to fight, but someone's got to do it. Because if I don't fight for me, who will? (Travis, Youth Researcher, essay excerpt)

As they developed a sense of individual and collective agency, the youth came to see their parents and grandparents in different lights, to appreciate the struggles that had been waged on their behalf, and to recognize their responsibility to carry the torch for the next generation. As Ashley explained:

Before researching the Achievement gap I had never heard of it. ... I never had the urge to make a change because my attitude was "that's just the way things are. ... Change was not realistic. Now that I know what the achievement gap is (or the title for it), I want to make a change. Our Mothers on the Move oral history project and interviewing the activists in my community has encouraged me to want to make a change. Listening to all of our parents and grandparents tell their stories of how they've struggled to make it better for us has made me want to get out there and help. I think this experience and project has widened my outlook on many things and issues. (Ashley, Youth Researcher, essay excerpt)

Just as MOM organizing helped their mothers view injustice as mutable, the PAR process enabled the youth to shatter the perceived inevitability of inequity. Shocking comparisons of schools, facilitated by trips to wealthy suburban school districts, analyses of school report cards, and statistical data from the U.S. Census and the National Coalition of Educational Activists, helped them to see disadvantage as related to race, ethnicity, and class, and oppression as systemic.

More specifically, in terms of our data, we found that by engaging in local organizing (for the mothers) and participatory research (for the youth), mothers and youth reframed private problems as public struggles (Mills, 1959); they reviewed social arrangements that once appeared intractable to be, now, mutable; they saw their own oppressive conditions as shared by many others; they understood themselves as agents able to deconstruct and challenge existing conditions; they voiced a sense of responsibility to those "left behind:"

> I knew 52 was a low performing school but when I saw the statistics, and that was really powerful they handed out information on the different schools in the area and we saw that there was a cluster of low performing schools right here in the southern part of the district yet District 8 encompasses the Sound View and Throggs Neck section. Throggs Neck which is mainly predominately White middle class and Sound View which is a mix in between here and there and you could see as the neighborhoods got better the scores the reading and math scores got better so that's when I knew we had to do something and meeting to talk with other people just I mean I knew I had to do something. (Ms. Chair, MOM board member, interview excerpt)

For Ms. Chair and Travis, their confrontation with data provided evidence of systemic inequity. The death of their (American) dream became the birth of their activism. Travis came to understand that "there was a word to describe my harsh experiences while attending public schools." Through the research, the youth began to review their disparate educational outcomes as unfair and transformable. They rejected the sense of inevitability, that this is "just the way things are," and began to see themselves as agents capable of creating "cracks in the cement."

Through what we have come to call the "power of the aggregate," mothers and youth reviewed patterns of data that allowed them to reject (exclusive) personal attributions (for student failure), and discern the historic, "racialized" and classed nature of educational inequity and the denial of equal opportunity. Christine noted that after she visited a privileged school, she came to understand that her miseducation was part of a larger history of race and class oppression:

> I was never really exposed to anything outside my community. It's hard to see that something is unjust if you haven't been to many other places. …I remember when I went to summer school one year and because I was late I didn't have a seat. I had to stand up in that hot ass un-air conditioned class for 45 minutes, or lean against a graffiti locker. So seeing Mamaroneck high school really made me mad, glad, and sad all at the same time. Mad because my school didn't look like that, the school was like a school you've seen on 90210 on TV. They had clean hallways, beautiful staircases and chandeliers to light the classrooms, while my schools couldn't compare. Glad because I am not in school anymore and I'm done with that … And sad for my kids who will have to go through that shit and the kids that are going through it now. (Christine, Youth Researcher, free writing after research training session)

Over the course of our participatory consultation, the youth came to recognize the need to educate the public and the next generation. Their "personal" stories were emblematic of a generation that had been unfairly denied; their stories were worthy of being elevated to "data," social analysis, and research. Travis wrote the following on his journey toward becoming a researcher:

> I first didn't think of myself as a researcher…I did not want to label myself as one either. I did not like researchers myself. I stereotyped researchers as being rich-know it-all's who learned of everyone else's problems, thought they were better than the people who were being researched/interviewed, and just could not relate to the experiences of the people who were being researched/interviewed. But the MOM oral history project changed all of that. I learned that anyone can be a researcher… And who better to research/interview inner-city parents and youth than myself…. It feels good also knowing that I'm not all alone in this and that I have supportive and influential women working besides me who also happen to be teenagers, which is great as well. (Travis, Youth Researcher, excerpt from a presentation at Teacher's College Winter Roundtable)

Viewing themselves as consultants to their mothers' and grandmothers' organization, the young people broadened their sense of responsibility for the educational justice to other youth.

As Jeunesse elaborated:

> Throughout this project my thoughts on educational injustice have changed. I've learned that even though you are getting treated fairly, you don't have to turn your back on people who are not. Many members of MOMs have children that are already in college but they are still fighting to make things right. Just because some issues aren't affecting you directly, doesn't mean they aren't hurting the people around you. (Jeunesse, Youth Researcher, essay excerpt)

DIFFICULTIES IN PARTICIPATORY CONSULTATION

Our consultation with MOM was premised on the expectation that a more refined understanding of the structural ingredients of the gap would stimulate a desire for collective action. We also assumed that there was an equivalence of meaning about what constituted action and change. We learned, however, that moving from critique to action is a complex and sometimes contradictory process, easier for some than for others. Learning about the race, ethnic, and class biases that constitute public education was empowering for some, but it was depressing for others. Jeunesse, educated and living in more privileged situations, digested the statistics and theory, and in rapid succession, grew to be critical and empowered:

> Kids should be taught about critical consciousness. They need to know what's going on at a young age so that when they get older the truth won't be a surprise to them. Growing up with prior knowledge about life is helpful so that kids can try to do something about it. They'll be able to be ready and tell their peers what's going on and maybe one day there will be a change. If everyone becomes critically conscious then things will not be the way they are now in the future. (Jeunesse, Youth Researcher, e-mail correspondence to Monique after research training session)

However, this process was more trying for those students who had been less educationally advantaged or were beaten up by the system. One of the youth researchers expressed her frustrations as follows:

> I'm not sure if I agree that teaching children about critical consciousness is a *great* idea. In many ways teaching children is good because they it prevents them from living with false consciousness, but some children may take what

they learn as there being no hope for their future and may not strive for their best. (Ashley, Youth Researcher, e-mail correspondence)

Ashley worries that critical knowledge can dampen the spirits of possibility that kindle within communities that have been economically and structurally abandoned by the private sector and the state. Travis suggested that the documentation of inequity and struggle can "rob children of their innocence:"

> I agree, but in the same token I disagree. Children should be taught at a young age critical consciousness because a generation filled with critically conscious children could spark a revolution for change in our world. But I disagree also because that spoils the childhood of alot of children. Their hopes are put on hold if not already diminished. (Travis, Youth Researcher, e-mail correspondence)

Interestingly, although we had presented our material at a variety of professional and community sessions, it was not until we presented to an audience of youth, in the Bronx, that all of the youth researchers felt engaged in action. That is, they needed to consult with peers to understand the power of their analyses.

Participatory consultation with youth requires behind the scenes supports, for example, taking time to forge real relationships with our coresearchers, magnificent supportive parents to call on, an amazing organization to fall back on, and funds to finance fun. Further issues emerged that may require consideration in similar projects. By working closely on the history, and with the youth, and by creating the Web site, we revealed the strengths of the organization and became an intimate part of organizational life. "Exit" strategies, thereby, proved difficult. There was always one more project on which we could be helpful. The resources that the Graduate Center brought—in terms of funds, research expertise, networks, and legitimacy in some circles—were critical to the sustenance of this organization.

Just as the youth researchers developed a rich sense of responsibility to sustain the educational dreams of all youth, so too we as consultants came to feel responsible to keep feeding such a wonderful, precious, unusual, and fragile organization in the South Bronx with the meager, but meaningful, financial and cultural capital that the Graduate Center had to offer.

Yet another struggle concerns the discrepancy between the youths' engagement with this work, and their own academic work. Although the young people were engaged energetically with our collective work, a number of them grew increasingly angered by the educational conditions they confronted. That is, they recognized that their excitement about learning did not translate into enthusiasm for their schools. To the contrary, there is, for a few, a transfer of anger and outrage at the miserable conditions called schooling in abandoned communities. Such outrage contributed to a retreat from education by a few of the youth—even as their mothers were fighting to reclaim educational possibilities.

FUTURE CONSULTATION

Inspired by the power of combining youth research and community organizing, we have been collaborating with a number of Public Education Network funds on their activist campaigns for public education. At "camps" for educators, organizers, parents, and youth from a number of districts, we have helped them design youth research and activism components to their campaigns. We have been most encouraged by our collaboration with MOM, and have been solicited by a number of community-based organizing groups for assistance in developing a youth PAR component. We have joined with youth activists and critical youth scholars to create a "diaspora" of youth research and consultation projects across the nation, a virtual social movement of youth research for social justice.

REFLECTIONS FOR CONSULTATION

This project affirms the power of consultative partnerships between universities, communities, and youth. Our collaboration documented across multiple generations illustrates how critical research can launch activism by youth, mothers, and grandmothers. Although much social psychological research has investigated the conditions under which critical consciousness can be provoked, few have studied the relation of consciousness to culture and fewer have studied the relation of consciousness to action (for exceptions, see Anand et al., 2002; Bookman & Morgan, 1988; Fine & Burns, 2003; Guishard, Doyle, et al., 2003; Guishard, Fine, et al., 2003; Naples, 1992; O'Connor, 1997; Ward, 2000; Watts & Abdul-Adil, 1999). The MOM consultation reveals how catalytic energy emerges when multiple generations come together to critique what is, to create what could be, and to produce a Web site (http://www.mothersonthemove.org) to be used for organizing future members—youth and mothers.

We close with the words of Ms. Sojourner who explained eloquently why parents must become "community mothers" (Naples, 1992) and activists for social justice, even after their children are grown:

> Well like I said my children, my daughter, my youngest child is in second year of college. I coulda stopped along time ago, but see I don't take my children I take all…I been living in this community for years so I take all the children in my community to be mine…because I would love to see my neighbor child graduate from college also because I don't have to see them on the corner where they setting him up cause that's what they do they fail our children and set them up for the jail so I will fight til' I cant fight no more as long as I you know as long as I got breath I'll fight for them cause they in my neighborhood and every child is mine. (Ms. Sojourner, MOM member, interview excerpt)

And now the mothers of MOM can breathe more easily, as they witness their children carry the torch into the next generation.

REFERENCES

Anand, B., Fine, M., Perkins, T., Surrey, D., & The Renaissance School Class of 2000. (2002). *Keeping the struggle alive: Studying desegregation in our town.* New York: Teachers College Press.

Anyon, J. (1997). *Ghetto schooling: A political economy of urban educational reform.* New York: Teachers College Press.

Bookman, A., & Morgan, S. (Eds.). (1988). *Women and the politics of empowerment.* Philadelphia: Temple University Press.

Bowles, S., & Gintis, H. (1976). *Schooling in capitalist society.* New York: Basic Books.

Brown v. Board of Educ., 347 U.S. 483 (1954).

Chataway, C. (1997). An examination of the constraints on mutual inquiry in a participatory action research project. *Journal of Social Issues, 53*(4), 747–766.

Clare, M. M. (2002). Diversity as an independent variable: Considerations for research and practice in consultation. *Journal of Educational and Psychological Consultation, 13,* 251–263.

Crenshaw, K., Sotanda, N., Peller, S., & Thomas, K. (Eds.). (1995). *Critical race theory: The key writings that influenced the movement.* New York: The New Press.

Crosby, F., Pufall, A., Snyder, R. C., O'Conell, M., & Whalen, P. (1989). The denial of personal disadvantage among me, you, and the other ostriches. In M. Crawford & M. Gentry (Eds.), *Gender and thought: Psychological perspectives* (pp. 79–96). New York: Springer-Verlag.

Deutsch, M. (1974). Awakening the sense of injustice. *Social Justice Research, 2,* 3–23.

Duncan, L. E. (1999). Motivation for collective action: Group consciousness as a mediator of personality, life experiences, and women's rights activism. Political socialization [Special issue]. *Political Psychology, 20*(3) 611–635.

Fals-Borda, O. (1979). Investigating reality in order to transform it: The Columbian experience. *Dialectical Anthropology, 4,* 33–55.

Fals-Borda, O., & Muhammad A. R. (1991). *Action and knowledge: Breaking the monopoly with participatory action research.* New York: Apex Press.

Ferguson, R. (1998). Can schools narrow the Black–White test score gap? In C. Jencks & M. Phillips. (Eds.), *The Black–White test score gap* (pp. 318–374). Washington, DC: Brookings Institute.

Fine, M. (1983). Social context and a sense of injustice: The option to challenge. *Representative Research in Social Psychology, 13,* 15–33.

Fine, M. (1991). *Framing dropouts: Notes on the politics of an urban high school.* Albany: State University of New York Press.

Fine, M. (2004). The power of the Brown v. Board of Education decision: Theorizing threats to sustainability. *American Psychologist, 59,* 502–510.

Fine, M., Bloom, J., Burns, A., Chajet, L., Guishard, M., Payne, Y., et. al. (2005). *Dear Zora: Reflections on Brown v. Board of Education, 50 years later.* Manuscript submitted for publication.

Fine, M., & Burns, A. (2003). Class notes: Toward a critical psychology of class and schooling. *Journal of Social Issues, 59*(4), 841–860.

Fine, M., Torre, M.E., Boudin, K., Bowen, I., Clark, J., Hylton, D., et. al. (2003). Participatory action research: Within and beyond bars. In P. Camic, J. E. Rhodes, & L. Yardley, (Eds.), *Qualitative research in psychology: Expanding perspectives in methodology and design* (pp. 173 198). Washington, DC: American Psychological Association.

Fine, M., & Wong, L. M. (1995). Freeing the compliant victim: Perspectives on (in)equity. In B.B. Bunker & J. Z. Rubin (Eds.), *Conflict, cooperation, and justice: Essays inspired by the work of Morton Deutsch* (pp. 315–349). San Francisco: Jossey-Bass.

Freire, P. (1970). *Pedagogy of the oppressed.* New York: Continuum.

Freire, P. (1973). *Education for critical consciousness.* New York: Continuum.

Freire, P. (1994) *Pedagogy of hope: Reliving pedagogy of the oppressed.* New York: Continuum.

Giroux, H. A. (1983). Ideology and agency in the process of schooling. *Journal of Education, 165,* 12–34.

Grant, P. R., & Brown, R. (1995). From ethnocentrism to collective protest: Responses to relative deprivation and threats to social identity. *Social Psychology Quarterly, 58,* 195–212.

Guishard, M., Doyle, C., Jackson, J,, Singleton, S., Staten, T., & Webb, A. (2003). *As long as I got breath, I'll fight: Participatory action research for educational justice. The family involvement network of educators, a Harvard family research project.* Retrieved May 5, 2003, from http://www.gse.harvard.edu/hfrp/projects/fine/resources/digest/par.html

Guishard, M., Fine, M., Doyle, C., Jackson, J., Staten, T., & Webb, A. (2005). *"See some people they don't have...the people or the organization who's interested to educate people and to let them know what does justices mean:" Understanding Lived critical consciousness nourished by community activism.* Unpublished master's thesis, The Graduate Center of the City University of New York, New York.

Gurin, P., Miller, A. H., & Gurin, G. (1980). Stratum identification and consciousness. *Social Psychology Quarterly, 43,* 30–47.

Hill-Collins, P. (1998). *Fighting words. Black women and the search for justice.* Minneapolis: University of Minnesota Press.

Hill-Collins, P. (2000). *Black feminist thought: Knowledge, consciousness, and the politics of empowerment* (2nd ed). New York: Routledge.

Hooks, B. (1994). *Teaching to transgress: Education as the practice of freedom.* New York: Routledge.

Jost, J., Pelham, B. W., Sheldon, O., & Sullivan, B. N. (2003). Social inequality and the reduction of ideological dissonance on behalf of the system. *European Journal of Social Psychology, 33,* 13–36.

Kemmis, S., & McTaggart, R. (2000). Participatory action research. In N. Denzin & Y. S. Lincoln (Eds.). *Handbook of qualitative research* (2nd ed., pp. 567–606). Thousand Oaks, CA: Sage.

Kozol, J. (1991). *Savage inequalities.* New York: Crown.

Lareau, A. (2003). *Unequal childhoods: Class, race, and family life.* Berkeley: University of California Press.

Lott, B. (2001). Low-income parents and the public schools. *Journal of Social Issues, 57*(2), 247–259.

Lott, B., & Bullock, H. (Eds.). (2001). Listening to the voices of poor women [Special issue]. *Journal of Social Issues, 57*(2).

Martín-Baró, I. (1994). *Writings for a liberation psychology.* Cambridge, MA: Harvard University Press.

Mills, C. W. (1959).*The sociological imagination.* New York: Oxford University Press.

Naples, N. A. (1992). Activist mothering: Cross generational continuity in the community work of women from low income urban neighborhoods. *Gender & Society, 6,* 441–463.

Nelson, N., Prilleltensky, I., & MacGillivary, H. (2001). Building value-based partnerships: Toward solidarity with oppressed groups. *American Journal of Community Psychology, 29,* 649–677.

New York ACORN Schools Office. (2000). *The secret apartheid: A report on racial discrimination against Black and Latino parents and children in the New York City public schools.* Retrieved August 15, 2000, from http://www.acorn.org/ACORNarchives/studies/secretapartheid /index.html

Nyc.gov. (2003). *My Neighborhood Statistics 928 Intervale Avenue.* Retrieved January 6, 2003, from http://gis.nyc.gov/ops/mmr/findlocation.jsp/street=928+intervale+avenue& borough=Bronx&geocodemode=1

O'Connor, C. (1997). Dispositional toward collective struggle and educational resilience in the inner city: A case analysis of six African American high school students. *American Educational Research Journal, 34,* 593–629.

Patton, M. Q. (2001). *Qualitative research and evaluation methods* (3rd ed., pp. 431–469). Newbury Park, CA: Sage.

Ransby, B. (2003). *Ella Baker and the Black freedom movement: A radical democratic vision.* Chapel Hill: University of North Carolina Press.

Reason, P. (1994). Three approaches to participative inquiry. In N. Denzin & Y. Lincoln (Eds.), *Handbook of qualitative research* (pp. 324–339). Thousand Oaks, CA: Sage.

Runciman, W. G. (1966). *Relative deprivation and social justice: A study of attitudes to social inequality in twentieth century England.* Berkeley: University of California Press.

The Brooklyn AIDS Task Force. (2003, June). *2003 Hunts Point/Mott Haven HIV/AIDS profile.* Retrieved August 15, 2003, from http://www.taclearinghouse.org/clearinghouse/re-source.nsf/0/ABCAB5C6CA1BAFE587256BDF005BA715/$file/2003%20Mott%20Have n.pdf?OpenElement

The Education Trust. (2001). *Achievement in America 2001.* Retrieved October 1, 2001, from http://www2.edtrust.org/EdTrust/Product+Catalog/data+disks.htm

United States Department of Education. (1983). *An open letter to the American people: A nation at risk: The imperative for educational reform.* Retrieved July 8, 2001, from http:// www.ed.gov/pubs/NatAtRisk/index.html

United States Department of Education, National Center for Education Statistics. (2000, August). *National Assessment of Educational Progress 1999 trends in academic progress: Three decades of student performance.* Retrieved September 15, 2002, from http:// nces.ed.gov/pubsearch/pubsinfo.asp?pubid=2000469

Ward, J. (20 J). Raising resisters: The role of truth telling in the psychological development of African American girls. In L. Weis & M. Fine (Eds.), *Construction sites: Excavating race, class, and gender among urban youth* (pp. 50–64). New York: Teachers College Press.

Watts, R., & Abdul-Adil, J. (1999). Promoting critical consciousness in young, African–American men. *Journal of Prevention and Intervention in the Community, 16*, 63–86.

Watts, R., Williams, N., & Jagers, R. (in press). Sociopolitical development and the making of African American activists. *American Journal of Community Psychology.*

Monique Guishard is a doctoral candidate in the Social-Personality Psychology program at the Graduate and University Center of the City University of New York. Her research interests are lived perspectives of the ontogeny of critical and social consciousness development, multiple and polyphonic consciousness, social movements, and resilience.

Dr. Michelle Fine is a Distinguished Professor of Psychology, Women's Studies and Urban Education at the Graduate Center of the City University of New York. Committed to participatory action research in schools, prisons, and communities, her writings focus on theoretical questions of social injustice: how people think about unjust distributions of resources and social practices, when they resist, and how such inequities are legitimated. Interested in the combination of quantitative and qualitative methods, as well as participatory action designs, Dr. Fine's writings also focus on questions of epistemology, methodology, and social change.

Christine Doyle is a Liberal Arts student at a community college in the City University of New York.

Jeunesse Jackson is a junior at Brooklyn Technical High School in New York City.

Travis Staten is a Criminal Justice student at a senior college in the City University of New York.

Ashley Webb is a junior at Fashion Industries High School in New York City.

JOURNAL OF EDUCATIONAL AND PSYCHOLOGICAL CONSULTATION, *16*(1&2), 55–74
Copyright © 2005, Lawrence Erlbaum Associates, Inc.

Engaging African American Parents in the Schools: A Community-Based Consultation Model

Danel A. Koonce
University of Rhode Island

Walter Harper, Jr.
Brown University

Although it has been well established that parental involvement in school is linked to positive outcomes for children, there are a myriad of issues that make it challenging for some African American families to engage school personnel in collaborative problem solving (e.g., Hill & Craft, 2003). Some of the barriers that decrease involvement include parents' poor school experiences, intimidation by school personnel, and inconvenient meeting times. When parents' initial advocacy efforts are not effective, we must seek alternative methods. A recommended method is the collaborative efforts of community-based social service agencies and school consultants to engage African American families in mutually beneficial partnerships with schools to facilitate successful academic careers for their children (Witty, 1982). In this article, we discuss the barriers that African American families face when attempting to collaborate with schools and describe a multiphase model for engaging African American families with school to effectively advocate for their children's needs. A case study is presented describing the use of this model with a student exhibiting behavior problems in school.

There is considerable evidence that parental involvement is related to positive education outcomes for children (Hill & Craft, 2003; Jimerson, Egeland, & Teo, 1999; Kao & Tienda, 1998). Such involvement at school and at home

---

Correspondence should be sent to Danel A. Koonce, Department of Psychology, University of Rhode Island, 10 Chafee Road, Suite 8, Kingston, RI 02881. E-mail: dkoonce@uri.edu

is associated with creating positive school climates and improving students' attitudes toward school, school competency, school attendance, and homework habits (Astone & McLanahan, 1991; Fantuzzo, Davis, & Ginsburg, 1995; Izzo, Weissberg, Kaspro, & Frendrich, 1999; Lareau, 1987; Marion, 1980). Additionally, parental involvement has a positive impact on social behavior and interactions among peers (Fantuzzo et al., 1995; Izzo et al., 1999; Marcon, 1999; Wetzel, 1991). This is particularly important for minority students who have been disproportionately disciplined and suspended from schools across the country (Brooks, Schiraldi, & Zeidenberg, 1999; Morrison & D'Incau, 1997). However, the research suggests that when parents are (a) involved in the discipline process, (b) informed of their roles in the educational process, and (c) encouraged to participate in their children's academic and social development, students' suspensions and inappropriate school behaviors decrease (Nweze, 1993).

Although strategies for improving parental involvement have gained considerable interest with educational policymakers, many public schools have not been able to institutionalize parent involvement programs with ethnically diverse families as partners (Feuerstein, 2000; Trotman, 2002). The adoption of federal legislation (e.g., the Goals 2000 Educate America Act of 1994, Individuals with Disability Education Act of 1997, and Title I of the Improving America's Schools Act of 1994) mandating educators to establish mutually beneficial partnerships with parents have only given practitioners and researchers a limited understanding of the factors that increase the involvement of ethnically diverse families in schools. The research suggests that public schools have not made the most of the assets of engaging African American parents as partners to address the needs of their children (Obgu, 1978). In fact, some public schools have contributed to decreasing parental involvement by taking away responsibilities that once belonged to parents (Wallis, 1995). For example, in an investigation that examined how parents of color felt toward their children's school, Calabrese (1990) found that parents believed they were not welcome. The parents reported a high degree of alienation and felt the teachers related to them in a hostile manner. These results suggest that some schools are resistant to implementing programs to increase parental involvement, which complicates the problem of institutionalizing parent participation. Other studies have shown that some Black parents report negative school experiences (McCaleb, 1994; Menacker, Hurwitz, & Weldon, 1988), intimidation by school personnel (Anderson, 1994; Harry, 1992), poor understanding of how to navigate the educational system (Rao, 2000), and requests for meetings at inconvenient times (Trotman, 2002; Weitock, 1991) as barriers contributing to low parental involvement.

Harry (1992) noted that African American parents reported feelings of isolation, alienation, disengagement, and an array of other negative feelings regarding interactions with personnel at their child's school. In their frustration and anger at the school, the parents voiced being treated like second-class citizens, promoting what Harry described as a deficit or pathological view of African American families. It is not surprising that the families responded by withdrawing from further interactions with school personnel. The foregoing situations are a call for educators to evaluate and understand the "sometimes idiosyncratic historical relationship between a particular school or school district and its parents, as well as how it relates to parents' existing involvement or noninvolvement" (Raffaele & Knoff, 1999, p. 454).

When some African American parents are faced with the challenge of their own negative experiences with schools and often have to dispel the misconception that they do not care about the education of their children, they are left with few resources to receive parity in educational opportunities (Prater, 2002). Even African American parents who are able to successfully resolve negative school experiences remain reluctant to exercise their legal rights when advocating for their children (Harry, Allen, & McLaughlin, 1995; Marion, 1980). Thus, for these parents to become knowledgeable about their rights and understand the context in which to exercise them, a neutral mechanism is required to involve those who are disengaged. Witty (1982) described one such mechanism in which African American parents and community organizations collaborated with schools to attain their goals. Community-based organizations are a valuable mechanism to bring educators and families together to improve interactions between ethnic minority families and the public schools.

COMMUNITY-BASED EFFORTS

The National Urban League (NUL) is the nation's oldest community-based organization instrumental in empowering African Americans to become well-educated, attain economic self-sufficiency, and eradicate barriers to sustain participation in the economic and social mainstream of the United States. Local affiliates of the NUL provide mental health services, educational opportunities, and a multitude of assistance programs in housing and employment. One of the goals of the NUL is to create an environment that promotes, supports, and sustains the academic and social development of youth and children by partnering with parents, teachers, school administrators, community leaders, businesses and other service providers.

The local affiliate of the NUL in Providence, RI, represents the community-based social service agency (CSSA) that served as the school-community partner in our consultation project. Additionally, the agency served as the source of referrals and the location where the parent training occurred in our consultation efforts with African American parents.

In recent years, the development of school-community partnerships designed to connect with parents who are socially and economically disadvantaged "has been strongly recommended by general and special educators at all levels as an essential element in any strategic model or framework designed to promote equitable, quality educational opportunities" (Ford, 2002, p. 163). The literature review provides some rich examples of home–school collaboration programs that have been successful in involving groups of parents historically disenfranchised from the educational system (Comer & Hayes, 1991; Gavin & Greenfield, 1998; Morris, 1999). The fundamental belief underlying these programs is that schools, parents, and students must adopt an ecological approach and commit to a plan that promotes change in the system.

From an ecological perspective, Rafaelle and Knoff (1999) have suggested that home–school collaboration should include the efforts of parents and school personnel, as well as the efforts of institutions in the community (i.e., businesses, social service agencies, religious institutions, civic organizations). They argued that the components are all as important in fostering, facilitating, and institutionalizing the values, norms, and interactions for positive relations between home and school. An example of a framework that incorporates public schools as part of the community is called the value-based partnership model.

Nelson, Amio, Prilleltensky, and Nickels (2000) proposed a value-based partnership that is rooted in community development and the implementation of prevention programs. The partnership involves linking multiple stakeholders to work with immigrant and refugee children and their families. Nelson et al. advocated the use of a six-step process for the implementation of effective prevention programs, including the following: (a) create partnerships, (b) clarify values and vision and derive working principles, (c) identify and merge the strengths of different partners and approaches, (d) define the problem collaboratively, (e) develop the prevention program collaboratively, and (f) research and evaluate collaboratively. They defined partnerships as "relationships between community psychologists and oppressed groups (and possibly other stakeholders); relationships that strive to advance the values of caring, compassion, community, health, self-determination, participation, power-sharing, human diversity, and social justice for oppressed groups" (p. 123).

One area that has not received a great deal of attention in the consultation literature is combining the efforts of CSSAs and school consultants to empower families in cooperative and innovative ways to become successful advocates for their children. Because CSSAs located in urban settings have a long and stable history of supporting families and bridging relations between the communities and other organizations, they are a safe space for families to develop the skills to interact with school personnel and help their children succeed in school (Ford, 2002; Raffaele & Knoff, 1999). Additionally, this type of partnership can bring together community leaders from different fields (i.e., school personnel, religious leaders, civic associations) in a nonthreatening environment to discuss how to establish an infrastructure for better parent and school interactions. Our work with urban children of color in the Providence, RI, public schools has led us to formulate a new model of engaging African American families in schools based on 3 years of consultation experiences.

A PROPOSED MODEL FOR CONSULTATION WITH AFRICAN AMERICAN FAMILIES

Our model focuses on developing a positive collaborative relationship with families who are faced with the challenge of effectively advocating for their children in the school system to gain equity in services. Our experiences in consulting with African American families have primarily focused on working with women who are heads of households and caretakers. More often than not, the female caretakers lack the emotional or financial support of the children's biological fathers and because of their own educational challenges, have had to obtain hourly employment without sufficient benefits or health insurance. Additionally, these parents have been viewed and labeled as "difficult" because they had a history of limited involvement in the schools, coupled with frustrating early attempts to advocate for their children. In many instances, their insights about their children were dismissed and because they felt that their influence was limited, they withdrew from their advocacy role. This phenomenon is not an uncommon experience for culturally diverse and low socioeconomic status families (Harry, 1992; Lareau & Shumar, 1996).

In the implementation of this model, we have found that dissatisfaction and ineffective advocacy efforts have left parents feeling disillusioned and helpless and they sought the support of a CSSA to obtain the needed services. It is important to acknowledge that the experiences of the African American families with whom we work are not representative of all African

Americans (i.e., low income, single, head of household) and the programmatic and systematic changes that occurred during our consulting efforts may not represent the outcomes arrived by others. However, the themes that emerged from our experiences may be representative of what families of color experience in their advocacy efforts with urban school systems.

The participants in the constellation dyad of this model consist of the consultee (i.e., parent–child dyad) and the consultants (i.e., a staff member of the CSSA and a school psychologist, who is hired as a consultant by the CSSA).[1] There are two fundamental tenets of the model that we believe are essential for understanding the practice of working with African American families. First, many African American families strongly believe in supporting one another and maintaining a positive family quality of life. Poston and her colleagues (2003) defined family quality of life as the following: "conditions where the family's needs are met, family members enjoy their life together as a family, and the family members have the chance to do things that are important to them" (p. 313). Therefore, we viewed the family as the consultee, and members' cultural traditions, beliefs, and experiences are respected. Moreover, the family is viewed as a system, in that the behavior of every member is related to and dependent on the behavior of all the others (Conoley, 1987; Nicholas & Schwartz, 1998). Thus, the interconnectedness of the family is acknowledged and it is recognized that change in any one part of the system will affect the other parts. Nicholas and Schwartz understood that the lives of individuals who comprise the family are linked together such that their behavior becomes a product of mutual influence. The relationship established is informal, setting the stage for building an alliance where the consultants accept the parent–child dyad where they are, listen respectfully to their points of view, and appreciate their attitudes.

The second fundamental tenet of the model acknowledges that many African American families want to build a positive relationship with professionals within the school system. However, these families may not be prepared or understand how to become involved in a manner that is valued by school personnel (i.e., attending conferences, volunteering in the classroom, supporting the actions of teachers at school) because of institutional policies (i.e., program or class placement decisions, challenging curriculum choices, removing an unqualified teacher) that make it difficult for

---

[1]Throughout this article, the consultant employed by the community-based social service agency (CSSA) is referred to as the CSSA consultant and the school psychologist hired as a consultant to the CSSA is referred to as the school consultant. When the term *consultants* is used, we are referring to the school and CSSA consultants.

parents and professionals to work collaboratively (Foster, Berger, & McLean, 1981).

For parents to be positively engaged, we propose that they need training to learn to navigate the school system. The training modules we devised involved the following: (a) understanding how the school system operates, (b) learning how to voice concerns about the children to teachers and administrators to gain support, (c) understanding the educational guidelines for parental involvement, and (d) understanding the mandates of special education. The model incorporates a training component with the goal of helping the parents understand the mutually beneficial outcomes of their involvement in their children's educational career and its impact on teachers' expectations and instructional practices.

The third fundamental tenet of the model is that forming a partnership with a CSSA builds (a) a trusting and collaborative relationship with the family, neighborhood, and other important community resources (i.e., school administrators, churches, businesses, etc.); (b) creates a collaborative context for consultation; and (c) identifies the stakeholders who are invested in the overall development and growth of each family. The CSSA serves as a member of the consultation dyad (i.e., consultant and consultee) and assists parents in working with the schools to identify the best services for their children. This dyadic relation represents the spirit of collaborative consultation proposed by Fine and Gardner (1994), where families and professionals work together by sharing the responsibilities of planning, problem solving, and implementation of the intervention. Through this process, parents are immersed with professionals modeling behaviors that benefit the parent through the development of "an increased sense of efficacy and enhanced problem solving skill" (Fine & Gardner, 1994, p. 295).

In theory, CSSAs are structured to meet the diverse needs of a multitude of individuals and their families, and possess trained specialists that can work collaboratively with psychologists and other school professionals to enable families to secure economic self-reliance, parity, power, and civil rights. However, when challenges within the school environment emerge, they may seek to hire a consultant who understands the complexities of organizational change and approaches consultation from a multilevel perspective. In this model, the school consultant had an ongoing relationship with the CSSA that involved providing staff in-service training to help them better serve adolescent mothers needing support to obtain educational services (i.e., returning to high school). This serves as an impetus for forming a partnership that has two tiers: (a) the referral process and (b) the consultation phases.

The Referral Process

The framework for engaging families involves structuring the CSSA to serve as the referral source; this represents the first tier of the partnership. Families that require assistance advocating for their children are internally referred to the CSSA consultant. Our experience working with families indicates that a majority of the referrals were generated within the CSSA. That is, the staff members within the CSSA referred cases to the CSSA consultant, who had experience as a classroom teacher and training as a counseling psychologist. As a means of formalizing this tier, it is important to note that in the initial development of this partnership, the staff members within the CSSA met with the consultants to streamline the referral process. The dialogue within this meeting helped representatives of the CSSA to feel more comfortable with the referral process and alleviated any unintended consequences of competing views or agendas held by the CSSA staff and administrators.

Our consultation goals are consistent with Gutkin and Curtis (1990) because we focus on solving the presenting problem of the client and increasing the consultee's (i.e., parents) ability to solve similar problems in the future. As such, we instructed the staff within the CSSA about identifying appropriate referrals for the school consultant. Referrals that we deemed appropriate for our consultation efforts included the following: (a) children presenting with behavioral or academic concerns that may have resulted in a suspension from school, and (b) parents unable to effectively resolve the children's presenting problem(s) through the school.

If an appropriate referral is generated and the parent is willing to meet with the CSSA consultant and the school consultant, we enter the second tier of the partnership, the consultation phases. This tier involves the school consultant working in concert with the CSSA consultant and the parent–child dyad. At this point, the consultee and the consultants begin to discuss the family structure and move into a process of problem solving by identifying and analyzing the concerns expressed by the parent and those that the appointed CSSA member presents.

Consultation Phases

What follows is a description of the three phases that parents go through from the problem identification interviews with the CSSA consultant through the consultation meeting with the school system. The three phases are as follows: (a) structuring, (b) training, and (c) engagement.

Structuring.   The structuring phase of the consultation resembles the first two stages of the eclectic model of family consultation that Brown, Pryzwansky, and Schulte (2001) referred to as initiating the contact and assessment of the problem(s). This phase addresses the children's needs without ignoring the broader family context. The emphasis is on supporting the parent in taking an active role in the process, as well as on strengthening interpersonal relations with the parents. Through the process (of three 1-hr structuring interviews [SI]), attempts are made to build bridges that link family roles, communication patterns, and decision making to instill healthy interdependence and connectedness within the family and among the consultants. Moreover, therapeutic support is extended to the family because challenging issues are likely to emerge in an attempt to identify the sources of the concerns that are presented during this phase. The school and CSSA consultant collaborate to assess the family's readiness for acceptance and further involvement in decision making. The objective is to move toward decreasing the family's reliance on the professionals and increasing their sense of control over their lives. As the families learn to access and gain control over important resources and have a voice in decision making, they obtain the skills needed to interact more effectively with others to become effective change agents in the settings in which they live and work (Dunst, Trivette, & Deal, 1988; Juras, Mackin, Curtis, & Foster-Fishman, 1997).

Training.   The training phase begins with the introduction of educational modules that require the families' active participation at the CSSA site. These educational modules are designed to teach the parents specific skills in the use of human relations strategies and the development of general behavioral management skills. Because it is important to evaluate where the parents are developmentally in the process of becoming independent advocates, the number and length of modules is not predetermined, but individualized to meet their needs.

Within this model, role playing and modeling provide excellent platforms for teaching parents about using behavioral management principles, understanding the dynamics of administrative meetings, asking questions, requesting meetings, and presenting themselves as informed decision makers. Additionally, this process helps the parents to develop some of the professional knowledge they will need to actively participate in meetings and to become acquainted with the paperwork of multidisciplinary meetings. After the modules have been presented, the immediate needs of the families have been met, and a clear set of goals have been identified, an additional assessment is made to determine the parents' readiness to interact with the school professionals. This assessment entails gauging the parents' interpersonal skills through their demonstration of skill attainment in several role-playing scenarios that require the parents to engage in explicit discussions about their concerns and the results they anticipate after meeting with school professionals.

Engagement.   The engagement phase typically entails coaching the parents to contact the school system by developing a script for them to use to arrange a meeting. The content of the script includes the purpose of their call, their plan to invite consultants to the meeting, and the times and dates of their availability for the prospective meeting. As this is a critical stage of the parents' development in their advocacy skills, we process the potential outcomes of their contact with the school system and follow up their contact with an independent call to the administrator of the school buildings. This independent call to the administrator is only made when a parent is confronted with a barrier in establishing a meeting at the school. In our consultation experiences, and consistent with Maher, Illback, and Zins (1984), the attainment of administrative sanction is critical in the establishment and maintenance of consultation services. Gaining administrative sanction also increases opportunities for a continuum of services in the school and strengthens the bond of future parental involvement. Our consulting experience within schools has led to establishing a formal relationship with the school administration to help administrators understand the role of the CSSA consultants in the community. The relationship that we have developed with a local public school has led to the delivery of a multitude of services (i.e., counseling services and conflict resolution workshops for the children and school staff, cultural arts programs and health workshops for the children).

After the meeting is confirmed, we accompany the parents to the initial meeting to reaffirm the partnership role and share accountability for the outcome. This represents the next step in the engagement phase, meeting with the school system or often the multidisciplinary team (MDT; school psychologist, social worker, other school personnel). In some instances, the families referred to the CSSA consultant are not facing a special education problem and we meet with the guidance counselor or social worker to identify resources within the community that may be more appropriate to address the needs of the children and their families.

In meeting with the MDT, we accept the role of peer collaborators and mediators while allowing the parents to orient the meetings using probes that were used in the educational modules. The familiarity of this sequence helps the parents see themselves as successful and competent. When necessary, we assert our knowledge to offer a different level of support to the parents. If subsequent meetings are warranted because of student-related problems, we form the consultation relationship with the respective teacher(s) using a less directive approach, such as taking some responsibility in the planning and implementation of a home–school intervention to maintain the advocacy role of the parents. Thus, the relationship between the parents and the consultants does not create dependency but continues to enhance the parents' skills to become independent advocates for their children, an approach supported by the literature (see Noell &Witt, 1996; Watson & Robinson, 1996). More prescriptive approaches are only used when the resolution of a student-related problem is resistant to intervention. In those cases, a specific behavioral or classroom plan has to be developed and its implementation supported by the expertise of the school consultant. In this model, the consultants had an ongoing relationship with some of the school personnel in schools where we provided services to families. Therefore, the school personnel had a vested interest in working closely with us in the development and implementation of interventions to avoid the duplication of any services. For example, if an intervention that was developed in collaboration with the parent(s) and school personnel during an MDT meeting proved to be ineffective, it was not unusual for a representative from the MDT to contact the consultants for assistance in planning an alternative set of interventions. In instances where we did not have an existing relationship with school personnel, we emphasized our role as peer collaborators and offered our availability to assist in developing effective support services for the family.

EXAMINING CSSA CONSULTATION REFERRALS

Our model for working with African American families expands on some of the traditional approaches designed to involve parents in the educational experiences of their children (Christenson & Cleary, 1990; Comer & Haynes, 1991; Hoover-Dempsey & Sandler, 1995). The objective is to move the parents from a passive to a more active level of involvement by forming mutually beneficial partnerships between the family, school, and community that are important for their children's healthy development and success in school.

Since we began using this model of engaging families, there have been a variety of referrals that comprised our caseload. Most of the cases were not families whose children were receiving special education services, but the children would have benefited from receiving support services (i.e., counseling, resource support for one academic area). The most frequent concern presented by the families is academic problems having behavioral manifestations both at home and at school. For example, in one case, the student demonstrated inconsistent work performance in school (such as one week completing all in-class assignments and the next week only completing the assignments in two classes). At home, the child's academic problem was evidenced by inconsistencies in completing the homework (such as failing to bring the assignment home or difficulty starting the assignment). Other referral concerns entailed children exhibiting behavior problems that were inconsistently attended to by the school or parents (i.e., sporadic attendance, bullying), and children manifesting skill deficits that became apparent at the conclusion of a grading period.

In many of these cases, there was a dysfunctional pattern of interactions between school personnel and the families that required mediation to resolve the referral concerns. On one hand, the judgmental teachers' attitudes about the parents may have contributed to creating barriers in communication. However, when parents failed to respond to teachers' requests for assistance, this led to halting a collaborative process. Regardless of the problems, most of the referral concerns seemed appropriate for this model of service delivery. The case, following, depicts the use of our model with a family that was representative of our caseload.

Case Study

Reggie was the 9-year-old son of a single mother. He was a third-grade student with average intellectual and language abilities attending a private school. Six months prior to the consultation relationship, Reggie's teacher repeatedly called his mother expressing concerns about his rate of work completion and behavior during transitions between subjects. Immediately prior to his mother contacting the CSSA, Reggie was asked by the principal to leave the private school. Reggie was transitioned to a public elementary school where he began having difficulties with transitions and his new teacher began calling Reggie's mother with concerns similar to his former teacher. The teacher also noted that Reggie was behind academically based on her initial evaluation. The teacher requested several meetings with Reggie's mother and after each meeting his mother felt dissatisfied because she believed her perspective was being discounted. The mother's perspective was that Reggie did have difficulty getting along with his peers; however, she felt that the other children in the classroom instigated the problems and it was the teacher's responsibility to deal with these issues and involve the parents of the other children to resolve the concerns. Additionally, the mother felt that the teacher was making recommendations that were not appropriate (i.e., retention or use of medication). Reggie's mother was already receiving services through the CSSA to obtain her General Education Diploma (GED). She met with her GED instructor to seek his advice regarding her difficulties with Reggie's teacher and he referred her to the CSSA consultant.

The SI was conducted with Reggie, his mother, and the consultants to discuss his school-related behaviors and any relevant family concerns. During the SI, Reggie's mother stated that her primary concerns were his hyperactivity and her inability to provide Reggie with the sustained academic support that he required. She also stated that Reggie had been on a stimulant medication before but it upset his stomach and made him lethargic. As a result, she discontinued the medication. Reggie stated that sometimes he was not able to control his behavior, but he was trying his best at school. In terms of his behavior, Reggie reported that other students teased him and he responded by kicking or hitting them.

During the SI, the mother reported that when she met with Reggie's teacher, she was never able to express her needs or told how she could help her son with his schoolwork. Reggie's teacher stated to her that he was intelligent but was behind academically and it would be best if he repeated the third grade. His mother's efforts to help Reggie with his homework were met with resistance; he would rush through the work and he was unwilling to complete additional worksheets to reinforce concepts he was learning.

Reggie and his mother identified three changes in his behavior that they wanted to address as part of the intervention phase. They were as follows: (a) completing his homework and additional workbook activities at home to reinforce his school work, (b) ignoring negative comments from his peers, and (c) following the teacher's directions and asking for help when necessary. Along with these objectives, the consultants suggested that it was important to evaluate Reggie's current level of academic functioning and to conduct observations of his classroom behavior in response to the teachers' concerns. The school consultant conducted a brief assessment of Reggie's academic skills based on work samples provided by his mother and current teacher. Due to the behavioral concerns expressed by his teacher, the school psychologist and principal at Reggie's school were conducting behavioral observations to obtain a better understanding of the significance of the presenting problems, and to obtain a baseline of his in-class behavior.

The consultants and Reggie's mother agreed that she required training in several areas. The training modules addressed the concerns that Reggie's mother expressed about effectively communicating with the teacher, defining her parental involvement role, and understanding the special education process. The consultants shared the delivery of the training modules, with the school consultant having extensive training in behavioral consultation, assessment, and interventions.

Case study results.   Reggie's mother contacted the school 2 weeks after her initial contact with the CSSA. A meeting was arranged that included Reggie's mother, the principal, Reggie's teacher, and the CSSA consultants. The teacher presented a series of Reggie's work samples that reflected delays in writing and math. Reggie's mother expressed her concerns about retention and the consultants shared outcomes about retaining children in elementary school. The principal and teacher emphasized retaining Reggie but they expressed a willingness to consider options other than retention. Because of time constraints involved in initiating an in-house psychoeducational referral at the end of the school year, a consensus was reached to have Reggie evaluated privately with an MDT meeting convened prior to the end of the school year. Although Reggie's mother knew that she had the right to initiate a referral through the school, she had insurance that would cover the cost of the evaluation and time was critical. The results of the private evaluation reflected a diagnosis of attention deficit hyperactivity disorder and suggested a trial of nonstimulant medication. Moreover, the evaluation results confirmed that Reggie was performing below grade level in math and reading.

On sharing the results of the evaluation with the principal, Reggie's mother requested that the MDT convene. In consultation with Reggie's mother and the consultants, the MDT agreed to develop a Section 504 Plan with accommodations that the teacher was willing to try. Reggie's below-grade-level performance suggested that he had not mastered several skill areas that were required for the third grade. For example, Reggie was not able to accurately comprehend or recall the relevant and descriptive details of a story from beginning to end. In the area of mathematics, Reggie was not able to demonstrate a conceptual understanding of mathematical operations by illustrating the relation between repeated multiplication and addition using models. The decision was made to retain Reggie pending a review of his skills at the beginning of the next school year. Additionally, the consultants identified a tutor to assist Reggie's mother in implementing homework strategies for her son. Two weeks after the MDT meeting, treatment effects were assessed through interviews with the teacher and Reggie's mother, and through observations conducted by the school psychologist.

A review of the baseline data regarding Reggie's in-class behavior indicated a significant decrease in retaliation type behaviors (i.e., hitting or kicking) in response to being teased. It was speculated that this result was partly due to the trial of the non-stimulant medication and an increase in his self-control skills. Approximately five-weeks following the MDT meeting, Reggie's mother, teacher, and Reggie convened for a meeting with the principal. The meeting was held after consulting with Reggie's pediatrician about his classroom behavior where it was agreed that an additional dosage of medication was needed in the afternoon.

The school consultant conducted a skills analysis to assess Reggie's progress in reading and math at home and to determine if he possessed the prerequisite skills to complete assignments at school. The analysis revealed Reggie was accurately completing the math problems he attempted, suggesting that he understood the underlying concepts. In terms of reading, Reggie's comprehension skills required cueing for him to correctly respond to questions posed to him. This information was shared with Reggie's teacher so that it could be transferred to the classroom instruction.

The results of this case study provide an indication of the successful application of a model for working with African American families to obtain educational and social support for their children. In our consultation work with families, all the outcomes are not as positive. Some of the outcomes of this model do not increase parental involvement or result in the attainment of educational or social support for the child. In fact, a number of our parent consultees were not able to maintain stability in their lives (i.e., unplanned pregnancy, maintaining unhealthy relationships, loss of employment) or experienced parenting difficulties resulting in their disengagement from the consultation relationship.

SUMMARY

The experiences herein illustrate the importance of several principles in working with African American families. First, the development of a personalized relationship with each family with professionals that they trusted who viewed the family as a system were important for the effectiveness of the consultation relationship (Dinnebeil & Rule, 1994). The foci of the intervention in this case were on the family and school system, not just the child. We found that helping the mother acquire better parenting (i.e., managing child's behavior at home) and advocacy skills facilitated the psychological and educational development of her child. Additionally, the school professionals appeared to be more willing to work with the mother as she became more assertive and knowledgeable about the services available for her child. Kratochwill and Bergan (1990) emphasized that difficulties in family functioning must be treated as a system during consultation because each member reciprocally influences the other members. Moreover, Harry (1992) suggested that when forming partnerships, an emphasis should be placed on developing individual relationships and providing one-on-one communication. In our experience, we learned that the existence of an ongoing communication throughout the consultation relationship was important for the families so that they could anticipate potential difficulties and limitations of the consultation relationship.

The second principle illustrated in the scenarios described earlier is that the training that the parents received to help them understand and interpret school policies and agendas was necessary to prepare them to become independent advocates for their children. There is evidence in the consultation literature that direct training of consultees in discreet skills that improve their competence in problem solving can lead to enhancing consultation outcomes (Zins, 1993). For example, Kohr, Parish, Neef, Driessen, and Hallinan (1988) provided training to parents in the use of socially validated communication skills before interacting with professionals. The results of the investigation demonstrated that the parents acquired the targeted behaviors during simulated conferences, generally applied some of the skills to actual conferences, and were satisfied with the training program. In our consultation relationships, we felt that the training modules were the key to enhancing the consultees' advocacy skills so that they could effectively respond to similar concerns with the schools in the future (Gutkin & Curtis, 1990). Zins (1993) suggested that during the enhancement of consultees' professional skills, when psychological knowledge and skills are shared between the consultant and consultee, a skills transference occurs that presumably leads to better treatment outcomes. The integrated goals of this framework are to instruct parents in the decision-making process, which leads to improved consultee self-efficacy and to empower parents to work actively on behalf of their children.

Last, creating an alliance with different individuals (i.e., school personnel, community leaders, service providers) helped to facilitate communication and understanding between the professionals involved in the family's life. The building of an alliance provides everyone with experiences for personal growth and constant support to the family when barriers to school-community relationships arise.

The consultation model presented here is intended to serve as an alternative method of involving African American families in the schools. It is unique because it taps the existing resources of CSSAs whose historical mission has been to secure economic self-reliance, parity, power, and civil rights for families of color. Additionally, working with African American families through CSSAs reinforces the idea that increasing parental involvement cannot be achieved by schools alone, but requires a combination of resources within the community, as well as organizational change, to deliver effective educational programs that produce positive student outcomes (Abrams & Gibbs, 2000; Rafaelle & Knoff, 1999).

School-community partnerships, particularly those that use the resources of CSSAs who partner with consultants, are not well established in the literature. We acknowledge that this model addresses some aspects of supporting African American families in their attempt to become more involved in the school environment. On the other hand, its applicability and use deserves discussion and further exploration to determine its soundness as an innovative practice.

REFERENCES

Abrams, L. S., & Gibbs, J. T. (2000). Planning for school change: School community collaboration in a full-service elementary school. *Urban Education, 35*, 79–103.

Anderson, M. G. (1994). Perceptions about behavioral disorders in African American cultures and communities. In R. L. Peterson & S. I. Jordan (Eds.), *Multicultural issues in the education of students with behavioral disorders* (pp. 93–104). Cambridge, MA: Brookline.

Astone, N. M., & McLanahan, S. (1991). Family structure, parent practices, and high school completion. *American Sociological Review, 56*, 309–320.

Brooks, K., Schiraldi, V., & Zeidenberg, J. (1999). *School house hype: Two years later*. Retrieved July 29, 2003, from Center on Juvenile and Criminal Justice Web site: http://www.cjcj.org

Brown, D., Pryzwansky, W. B., & Schulte, A. C. (2001). *Psychological consultation: Introduction to theory and practice*. Boston: Allyn & Bacon.

Calabrese, R. L. (1990). The public school: A source of alienation for minority parents. *Journal of Negro Education, 59*, 148–154.

Christenson, S. L., & Cleary, M. (1990). Consultation and the parent-educator partnership: A perspective. *Journal of Educational & Psychological Consultation, 1*, 219–241.

Comer, J. P., & Hayes, N. M. (1991). Parent involvement in schools: An ecological approach. *The Elementary School Journal, 91*, 271–277.

Conoley, J. C. (1987). Schools and families: Theoretical and practical bridges. *Professional School Psychology, 2*, 191–203.

Dinnebeil, L. A., & Rule, S. (1994). Congruence between parents' and professionals' judgments about the development of young children with disabilities: A review of the literature. *Topics in Early Childhood Special Education, 14*(1), 1–25.

Dunst, C. J., Trivette, C. M., & Deal, A. (1988). *Enabling and empowering families: Principles and guidelines for practice*. Cambridge, MA: Brookline.

Fantuzzo, J. W., Davis, G. Y., & Ginsburg, M. D. (1995). Effects of parent involvement in isolation or in combination with peer tutoring on student self-concept and mathematical achievement. *Journal of Educational Psychology, 87,* 272–281.

Feuerstein, A. (2000). School characteristics and parent involvement: Influences on participation in children's schools. *The Journal of Educational Research, 94,* 29–40.

Fine, M. J., & Gardner, A. (1994). Collaborative consultation with families of children with special needs: Why bother? *Journal of Educational & Psychological Consultation, 5,* 283–308.

Ford, B. A. (2002). African American community resources: Essential education enhancers for African American children and youth. In F. E. Obiakor & B. A. Ford (Eds.), *Creating successful learning environments for African American learners with exceptionalities* (pp. 159–173). Thousand Oaks, CA: Corwin Press.

Foster, M., Berger, M., & McLean, M. (1981). Rethinking a good idea: A reassessment of parental involvement. *Topics in Early Childhood Special Education, 1*(3), 55–65.

Gavin, K. M., & Greenfield, D. B. (1998). A comparison of levels of involvement for parents with at-risk African American kindergarten children in classrooms with high versus low teacher encouragement. *Journal of Black Psychology, 24,* 403–417.

Goals 2000: Educate America Act. (1994). Pub. L. 103-227, 20 U.S.C. 5801 et seq.

Gutkin, T. B., & Curtis, M. J. (1990). School-based consultation: Theory, techniques, and research. In C. R. Reynolds & T. B. Gutkin (Eds.), *The handbook of school psychology* (2nd ed., pp. 577–611). New York: Wiley.

Harry, B. (1992). Restructuring the participation of African–American parents in special education. *Exceptional Children, 59,* 123–131.

Harry, B., Allen, N., & McLaughlin, M. (1995). Communication versus compliance: African–American parents' involvement in special education. *Exceptional Children, 61,* 364–377.

Hill, N. E., & Craft, S. A. (2003). Parent-school involvement and school performance: Mediated pathways among socioeconomically comparable African American and Euro–American families. *Journal of Educational Psychology, 95,* 74–83.

Hoover-Dempsey, K. V., & Sandler, H. M. (1995). Parental involvement in children's education: Why does it make a difference? *Teachers College Record, 97,* 310–331.

Improving America's School Act of 1994, Title I – Helping Disadvantaged Children Meet High Standards (1994).

Individuals with Disabilities Education Act (IDEA) Amendments of 1997 (1997). 20 U.S.C. 1400 et seq. Office of Special Education and Rehabilitive Services, Department of Education.

Izzo, C. V., Weissberg, R. P., Kaspro, W. J., & Frendrich, M. (1999). A longitudinal assessment of teacher perceptions of parent involvement in children's education and school performance. *American Journal of Community Psychology, 27,* 817–839.

Jimerson, S., Egeland, B., & Teo, A. (1999). A longitudinal study of achievement trajectories: Factors associated with change. *Journal of Educational Psychology, 91,* 116–126.

Juras, J. L., Mackin, J. R., Curtis, S. E., & Foster-Fishman, P. G. (1997). Key concepts of community psychology: Implications for consulting in educational and human service setting. *Journal of Educational & Psychological Consultation, 8,* 111–133.

Kao, G., & Tienda, M. (1998). Educational aspirations of minority youth. *American Journal of Education, 106,* 349–384.

Kohr, M., Parish, J. M., Neef, N. A., Driessen, J., & Hallinan, P. (1988). Communication skills training for parents: Experimental and social validation. *Journal of Applied Behavior Analysis, 21,* 21–30.

Kratochwill, T. R., & Bergan, J. R. (1990). *Behavioral consultation in applied settings: An individual guide.* New York: Plenum.

Lareau, A. (1987). Social class differences in family–school relationships: The importance of cultural capital. *Sociology of Education, 60*, 73–85.

Lareau, A., & Shumar, W. (1996). The problem of individualism in family-school policies. *Sociology of Education, 23*, 24–39.

Maher, C. A., Illback, R. J., & Zins, J. E. (Eds.). (1984). *Organizational psychology in the schools: A handbook for professionals.* Springfield, IL: Thomas.

Marcon, R. A. (1999). Positive relationships between parent school involvement and public school inner-city preschoolers' development and academic performance. *School Psychology Review, 28*, 395–412.

Marion, R. L. (1980). Communicating with parents of culturally diverse exceptional children. *Exceptional Children, 46*, 616–623.

McCaleb, S. P. (1994). *Building a community of learners: A collaboration among teachers, students, families, and community.* Hillsdale, NJ: Lawrence Erlbaum Associates, Inc.

Menacker, J., Hurwitz, E., & Weldon, W. (1988). Parent–teacher cooperation in schools serving the urban poor. *The Clearing House, 62*, 108–112.

Morris, J. E. (1999). A pillar of strength: An African American school's communal bonds with families and community since Brown. *Urban Education, 33*, 584–605.

Morrison, G. M., & D'Incau, B. (1997). The web of zero-tolerance: Characteristics of students who are recommended for expulsion from school. *Education and Treatment of Children, 20*, 316–335.

Nelson, G., Amio, J. L., Prilleltensky, I., & Nickels, P. (2000). Partnerships for implementing school and community prevention programs. *Journal of Educational & Psychological Consultation, 11*, 121–145.

Nicholas, M. P., & Schwartz, R. C. (1998). *Family therapy: Concepts and methods* (4th ed.). Boston: Allyn & Bacon.

Noell, G. H., & Witt, J. C. (1996). A critical re-evaluation of five fundamental assumptions underlying behavioral consultation. *School Psychology Quarterly, 11*, 189–203.

Nweze, B. (1993). *Increasing parent involvement, student attendance and appropriate school behavior of at-risk middle school students through parent partnerships.* Unpublished manuscript, Nova Southeastern University, Ft. Lauderdale, FL.

Ogbu, J. (1978). *Minority education and caste: The American system in cross-cultural perspective.* San Francisco: Academic.

Poston, D. J., Turnbull, A. P., Park, J., Mannan, H., Marquis, J., & Wang, M. (2003). Family quality of life outcomes: A qualitative inquiry launching a long-term research program. *Mental Retardation, 41*(5), 313–328.

Prater, L. P. (2002). African American families: Equal partners in general and special education. In F. E. Obiakor & B. A. Ford (Eds.), *Creating successful learning environments for African American learners with exceptionalities* (pp. 145–157). Thousand Oaks, CA: Corwin Press.

Raffaele, L. M., & Knoff, H. M. (1999). Improving home–school collaboration with disadvantaged families: Organizational principles, perspectives, and approaches. *School Psychology Review, 28*, 448–466.

Rao, S. S. (2000). Perspectives of an African American mother on parent-professional relationships in special education. *Mental Retardation, 38*(6), 475–488.

Trotman, M. F. (2002). Involving the African American parent: Recommendations to increase the level of parent involvement within African American families. *Journal of Negro Education, 70*, 275–285.

Wallis, S. (1995). Forced parental involvement. *The Education Digest, 60*, 21–25.

Watson, T. S., & Robinson, S. L. (1996). Direct behavioral consultation: An alternative to traditional behavioral consultation. *School Psychology Quarterly, 11*, 267–278.

Weitock, T. (1991). *The development and implementation of a parent outreach program to increase school involvement of fourth grade parents.* Unpublished manuscript, Nova Southeastern University, Ft. Lauderdale, FL.

Wetzel, K. R. (1991). Relations between social competence and academic achievement in early adolescence. *Child Development, 62,* 1066–1078.

Witty, E. P. (1982). *Prospects for black teachers: Preparation, certification, employment.* Washington, DC: ERIC Clearinghouse on Teacher Education (ERIC Document Reproduction Service No. ED 213 659)

Zins, J. E. (1993). Enhancing consultee problem-solving skills in consultative interactions. *Journal of Counseling and Development, 72,* 185–190.

Danel A. Koonce received his doctorate from the school psychology program at Oklahoma State in 2000 and is an Assistant Professor of School Psychology at the University of Rhode Island. His primary research interests are decision making in the diagnosis of disruptive behavior disorders, academic interventions for juvenile delinquents in alternative school settings, and designing and implementing services for socioculturally diverse families and their children.

Walter Harper, Jr., is a consultant and public health educator for a community-based service organization in Providence, Rhode Island. He received a master's degree from Loyola University with a concentration in Counseling Psychology in 1978 and a master's degree in Anthropology from Brown University in 1996. His areas of professional interest include HIV and AIDS prevention services, adolescent sexual health and family planning, minority health and wellness, educational needs of minority children, and designing and implementing services for socioculturally diverse families and their children.

JOURNAL OF EDUCATIONAL AND PSYCHOLOGICAL CONSULTATION, 16(1&2), 75–94

Assisting Parents of Bilingual Students to Achieve Equity in Public Schools

Salvador Hector Ochoa

Texas A&M University

Robert L. Rhodes

New Mexico State University

This article provides school-based consultants with an overview of the English language learner (ELL) student population and common programs available to ELL students (such as English-only programs, pull-out English as a second language [ESL], content-based ESL, transitional bilingual programs, maintenance bilingual programs, and two-way or dual language bilingual education programs). Past and current research examining bilingual education programs and guidelines and recommendations for the application of bilingual education knowledge to consultative practice with school personnel and culturally and linguistically diverse parents are discussed. Because of the paucity of research regarding school-based consultation related to bilingual education issues, guidelines and recommendations are presented within the larger framework of multicultural and cross-cultural consultation. Recommendations for future research regarding school-based consultation related to bilingual education issues are provided.

Most school personnel and mental health professionals are well aware that the U. S. population is becoming more ethnically diverse. This trend is clearly documented by the 2000 U.S. Census, which found that 37.3% of the U.S. population is comprised of individuals from culturally diverse back-

---

Correspondence should be sent to Salvador Hector Ochoa, PhD, Texas A&M University, TAMUS Mail Stop #4225, College Station, Texas 77843–4225. E-mail: shochoa@tamu.edu

grounds. One critical factor that has not received sufficient consideration is the number of individuals who are also from linguistically diverse backgrounds. Children who evidence limited or no English language skills are referred to as English language learners (ELL). The ELL student population (3.7 million) constitutes 8% of all pupils enrolled in U.S. public schools (Kindler, 2002). If demographic trends continue at their current rate, the ELL student population is expected to continue to grow at dramatic rates. The National Clearinghouse for English Language Acquisition (NCELA; 2002b) reported that the growth of the ELL student population increased by 105% during the 1990s alone.

The ELL student population is made up of pupils who speak more than 400 different languages (Kindler, 2002) and the top five language groups are Spanish, Vietnamese, Hmong, Haitian Creole, and Korean (NCELA, 2002a). Seventy-seven percent of the ELL population is comprised of Spanish speakers, whereas the remaining top four languages each constitute 2% or less (NCELA, 2002b).

An important factor to note is that many ELL students and their parents are recent immigrants to the United States. In fact, 20% of school-age children in the United States have one parent who was not born on American soil (U.S. Census Bureau, 2001). Nearly 90% of first-generation immigrant pupils "do not speak English at home" (Hernandez & Darke, 1999, p. 58). This is also true for nearly 60% of second-generation immigrant children (Hernandez & Darke, 1999). Moreover, approximately one third of parents of first-generation children have had a limited number of years of schooling (e.g., "8 or fewer years of education;" Hernandez & Darke, 1999, p. 103).

These data have significant implications for school consultants. In addition to the language barriers present in the consultation process as consultants work with ELL students and their families, the heterogeneity of the ELL student population presents additional challenges to school consultants due to the numerous different behavioral norms, cultural customs, and previous schooling practices across these 400 or more different language groups. Moreover, given that a significant number of ELL students are from first- and second-generation immigrant families, it is important for mental health and school-based consultants to recognize that the parents of these children may not understand how American schools operate or be aware of the various educational programs (e.g., bilingual education) available to assist their children. For consultants to assist these families in achieving equity within the public schools, it is important for them to understand key considerations and approaches to educational programming. Once consultants acquire this knowledge base, they can more effectively consult with parents to enable them to better understand their rights and opportunities and assist them in the selection of a program of choice for their child.

School-based consultants can also help culturally and linguistically diverse families achieve equity by providing services to school personnel (e.g., teachers, administrators, school counselors) who work directly with ELL students. Data indicate that a significant number of schools and teachers will be faced with educating ELL students. According to the National Center for Educational Statistics (NCES; 1997), nearly one in every two schools had ELL students. The NCES (2002) found that two in five teachers in the United States taught ELL students during the 1999 to 2000 school year.

Unfortunately, schools and teachers have not been successful in helping ELL students achieve equitable educational outcomes. Kindler (2002), for example, reported that only 16% and 30% of ELL students "assessed scored above the state-established norm" on English and Spanish reading tests, respectively (p. 8).

To help school-based consultants provide consultation services to parents of ELL students and school personnel involved with educating ELL students, the foci of this article is twofold. The first focus includes an overview of the programs potentially available for ELL students to help consultants develop a working knowledge of specific issues in the field. The second focus discusses how consultants can apply this knowledge to their work with culturally and linguistically diverse families and school personnel involved with educating ELL students.

PROGRAMS AVAILABLE FOR ELL STUDENTS

There are several different educational programs used to educate ELL students in the United States. These approaches include the following: English-only programs, pull-out English as a second language (ESL), content-based ESL, transitional bilingual programs, maintenance bilingual programs, and two-way or dual language bilingual education programs. These approaches vary in the amount of English and native language that is used for instructional purposes. A review of the literature for each of these different approaches also is discussed.

Some school personnel believe that it is best to educate ELL students in an English-only program in which all instruction occurs with English-speaking students in a general education classroom (Porter, 1998). This approach is advocated by educators and school-based practitioners who believe that for ELL students to learn English, they need to hear it and use it in an academic immersed setting. Parents who elect to place their children in this instructional setting do so for a variety of reasons. For example, some are encouraged or persuaded by school personnel to place their children in this setting because it is anticipated that they will learn English more quickly. In these and other situations, some culturally diverse families will not question the school's recommendation because they believe it is a form of disrespect (Roseberry-McKibbin, 2002). Other parents will select this arrangement because they have experienced firsthand the difficulty, and, perhaps even discrimination, associated with not being able to speak English. They do not want their child to encounter what they have experienced and prefer programs that will focus on teaching English to their children. Some of those parents also feel that they can continue the native language at home whereas the school can concentrate on teaching their children English.

A second approach used to instruct ELL students are ESL programs. One type of ESL is a pull-out ESL program. This approach attempts to facilitate the student's English proficiency and does not directly focus on academic content (Antunez & Zelasko, 2001). In this type of ESL program, the child is typically pulled out of his general education class to have a more individualized focused on English language development. Some ESL programs also use a push-in approach where the ESL teacher pulls out the students for part of the day and then pushes them into the classroom to work with the students within the classroom setting and with the classroom teacher. A second form of ESL is a content-based ESL program in which pupils receive "…instruction that is structured around academic instruction content rather than generic English language skills" (August & Hakuta, 1998, p. 6). The amount of time that the ELL students spend in an ESL program will vary with the personnel resources that are available. For example, some rural and urban school districts are unable to find a sufficient number of ESL certified teachers. In these situations, an ELL student might receive ESL services once a week for 30 min. This is in contrast to other ELL students who receive ESL services daily. An important factor to note is that ESL can be a stand-alone program that is offered to assist ELL students. When an ESL program is provided in this manner, it is the sole program they receive to address their linguistic needs. An ESL program is also typically incorporated into the three types of bilingual education programs (transitional, maintenance, and two-way; Baca, 2004).

Educators who support ESL pull-out programs stress the need for ELL students to learn English language skills (Brisk, 1998). Educational personnel who support the use of a content-based ESL program acknowledge that it is important to make instructional adjustments based on the ELL student's English language abilities. Simultaneously, they stress the importance of ELL students being exposed to instructional material to reduce the probability that they do not fall behind in acquiring important educational concepts. Both types of ESL programs emphasize learning English exclusively.

Other educational personnel believe that equity can best be achieved for ELL students and their families by providing instruction in their native language and in English. One instructional method that uses native and English language instruction is transitional bilingual education (TBE) programs. TBE programs provide instruction in both English and the child's first language. The key feature of a TBE program is that instruction is provided in both languages, but only for a short period of time. This program usually exists for 2 to 3 years (kindergarten through second or third grade; Baca, 2004). As ELL students proceed through this program, the amount of instructional time in English is increased and instructional time in the child's native language is decreased. ELL students are often administered language proficiency tests to determine if they have met exiting criteria. Educators who support the use of TBE programs believe that it is important to initially provide instruction in the child's native language to ensure that the child comprehends and masters the academic content (Ovando & Collier, 1998). Some educators who support this program also believe that the length of time (e.g., number of years) that both languages are used should be limited because the children will otherwise never stop relying on their native language skills and fully develop or rely on their English language skills.

Another form of bilingual education is a maintenance program. Similar to the TBE program, a maintenance program also uses both the child's native language and English (August & Hakuta, 1998). Maintenance programs differ from TBE programs in the number of years that both languages are used for instructional purposes. Maintenance programs utilize both languages for approximately 5 to 6 years (Baca, 2004). The amount of instruction in the native language is about 80% to 90% in kindergarten and in first grade and gradually reduces as the child proceeds to the higher elementary grades (Antunez & Zelakso, 2001). In some programs, a balance of native language and English is continued to maintain both languages. Educators who support this approach claim that this program enables ELL students to learn English while maintaining their first language (August & Hakuta, 1998). This does not occur in an English-only program, either type of ESL program, or in a TBE program because the child is expected to learn English and not maintain his or her first language. Educators and researchers who advocate using this approach believe that as a result of maintaining their first language while acquiring English, ELL students will achieve educational equity when compared with English-speaking peers (Thomas & Collier, 1997, 2002).

Another instructional program that is used to educate ELL students in U.S. schools is a two-way or dual bilingual program. Two-way bilingual programs are very similar to maintenance programs with respect to the number of years that instruction is provided in both English and a second language. A distinguishing feature of two-way bilingual program classrooms is that they are comprised of both ELL students and native English speakers with both English and a second language used as the mediums for instruction (Antunez & Zelasko, 2001). Thus, ELL students are acquiring English, whereas native English speakers are learning a second language (Feinberg, 2002). Two-way bilingual programs are considered to be enrichment programs and are typically viewed favorably by educators and families (Crawford, 1999). Many English-speaking parents recognize the potential future employment benefits of having their child learn an additional language (Liu & Fern, 2003; NCELA, 1996). Parents of ELL students are often relieved to note that their native language and culture is valued because families from English-speaking backgrounds have elected to have their child participate in the program. Moreover, they recognize that their child will not be segregated from his or her English-speaking peers.

RESEARCH EXAMINING PROGRAMS FOR ELL STUDENTS

Several comprehensive studies (i.e., Ramirez, Yuen, & Ramey, 1991; Thomas & Collier, 1997, 2002) have examined the effectiveness of educational programs for ELL students. Several studies have used different methodological approaches. For example, some studies have used a vote-counting methodology (Baker & de Kanter, 1981, 1983; Rossell & Baker, 1996; Zappert & Cruz, 1977) whereas others have used a meta-analysis approach (Greene, 1998; Willig, 1985). Vote-counting studies examine whether the results of a series of investigations pertaining to a similar topic are statistically significant. If significant results were not obtained, the study is assigned to a neutral category. If significant results were obtained, the study is given a positive vote if the experimental group (bilingual education) is significantly greater than the control group (not in bilingual education) or a negative vote if the control group is significantly greater than the experimental group. The researcher totals the neutral, positive, and negative votes across these series of investigations to reach conclusions about the effectiveness of various programs. A meta-analysis approach

> involves translating the findings of a set of related studies into "effect sizes." …. By calculating an effect size for every relevant study in your review, you are translating the various results into a comparable unit of measure …which can be averaged in order to give you a composite quantitative estimate of the results of the studies you have reviewed. (Borg, 1987, p. 95)

Significant limitations have been identified as associated with a vote-counting methodology (see Greene, 1998; Thomas & Collier, 1997; Willig, 1985). The vote counting procedure's "greatest weakness is that it considers only the direction of the effect for each study and includes no estimate of its magnitude (Borg & Gall, 1989, p. 171).

Meta-analysis studies have found that bilingual education is an effective instructional approach to use with ELL students when compared to English immersion programs (Greene, 1998; Willig, 1985). Willig (1985) reported a mean effect size of .63 favoring bilingual education programs, which "indicate[s] that the average student in bilingual education programs scored higher than 74% of the students in the traditional programs when all test scores were aggregated" (p. 291). Willig found that "positive effect of bilingual education … were found for all major academic subjects whether tests were administered in English or in other languages…" (p. 297). Greene (1998) concluded as follows: "Despite the relatively small number of studies, the strength and consistency of these results, especially from the highest quality randomized experiments, increases confidence in the conclusion that bilingual programs are effective at increasing standardized test scores in English" (p. 4).

Some studies have compared the effectiveness of different types of bilingual education programs in general and across grade levels (Ramirez, et al., 1991; Thomas & Collier, 1997, 2002). Ramirez et al. (1991) compared the academic performance of ELL students enrolled in English immersion, TBE, and maintenance programs and found positive outcomes for students enrolled in maintenance programs. However, ELL students enrolled in English immersion and TBE did not fare as well. Thomas and Collier (1997) found that ELL students enrolled in two-way bilingual education and maintenance programs evidenced positive educational outcomes as they obtained normal curve equivalent (NCE) scores of 61 and 52 "on standardize tests in English reading,", respectively, at 12th grade (Thomas & Collier, 1997, p. 52). These findings indicate that ELL students enrolled in these two types of bilingual programs were at or above the national average with respect to their English reading abilities. ELL students enrolled in TBE and ESL pull-out and content programs did not evidence positive educational outcomes at 12th grade. ELL students in ESL pull-out and content programs attained NCE scores of 34 and 24 "on standardized tests in English reading," respectively, at 12th grade (Thomas & Collier, 1997, p. 52). Thomas and Collier (2002) also found positive educational outcomes for ELL students enrolled in two-way and maintenance programs and did not find favorable results for students in TBE and ESL programs. Based on their findings, Thomas and Collier concluded the following:

> Students with no proficiency in English must not be placed in short-term programs of only 1 to 3 years. In this study and all other research studies following ELL students long term, the minimum length of time it takes to reach grade level performance in L2 [English] is 4 years.... Parents who refuse bilingual/ESL services for their children should be informed that their children's long-term academic achievement will probably be much lower as a result, and they should strongly be counseled against refusing bilingual ESL services when their child is eligible. (p. 5)

It is important to acknowledge that bilingual education research shows that children in maintenance bilingual programs catch up to their peers in terms of English proficiency and functioning, but this usually takes them longer than 4 years. Thomas and Collier (1997) found that ELL students in maintenance bilingual programs do catch up to their English speaking peers by approximately the sixth grade. Thomas and Collier (1997) also found that "it takes" ELL students instructed only in English "7–10 years or more to reach the 50th NCE, and the majority of these students do not ever make it to the 50th NCE, unless they receive support for L1 [native language] academic and cognitive development at home" (p. 36).

Many of the research studies examining the effectiveness of programs available for ELL students are not included in this review due to methodological weaknesses. Some of the limitations noted for studies in this area include the following: (a) lack of information regarding implementation fidelity (O'Malley, 1978), (b) failure to differentiate among the various types of programs offered (Weaver & Padron, 1999), (c) short-term nature of the investigations (Thomas & Collier, 2002), and (d) lack of control "for differences between students assigned to bilingual programs and students assigned to English-only control groups" (Greene, 1998, pp. 2–3). Consultants reviewing research in this area should be aware of these limitations.

APPLYING BILINGUAL EDUCATION KNOWLEDGE
TO CONSULTATIVE PRACTIVE

Although the American Psychological Association (APA; 2003) has established guidelines in multicultural education, training, practice, and organizational change, there is a paucity of research and literature related to the application of bilingual education knowledge to consultative practice. As a result, the transformation of knowledge to practice is typically the culmination of a labor-intensive information-gathering process on the part of individual consultants. An understanding of bilingual education, related research, and recommended practice as outlined provides the details necessary to begin the process. To complete the process of transforming knowledge to practice, several important topics must be addressed. The following section provides an overview of key concepts and concerns that should be clearly understood about bilingual education by school-based consultants. The intended recipients of consultative services, either school personnel or culturally and linguistically diverse parents and families, are specified within each area and recipient-specific recommendations are included.

UNDERSTANDING OF MULTICULTURAL AND
CROSS-CULTURAL CONSULTATION IN THE
SCHOOLS

Although school-based consultation involving bilingual education issues is not specifically addressed in the literature, the larger framework of multicultural and cross-cultural consultation provides a context for practice. Tarver Behring and Ingraham (1998, p. 58) defined multicultural consultation as "a culturally sensitive, indirect service in which the consultant adjusts the consultation services to address the needs and cultural values of the consultee, the client, or both." Cross-cultural consultation is a subset of multicultural consultation and happens when consultation occurs across cultures (Ingraham, 2000). School-based consultants providing services related to bilingual education need to have a working knowledge of the general principles of multicultural consultation as well as the ability to apply these principles in their practice with families from cultural and linguistic backgrounds that may differ from their own.

Ingraham (2000) proposed a Multicultural School Consultation (MSC) framework for selecting the appropriate approach when working with culturally and linguistically diverse families. The MSC framework is a guide to culturally appropriate school-based practice and may be utilized by both internal and external consultants using a variety of models (e.g., behavioral, ecological, instructional, mental health). The MSC framework is comprised of five components that are designed to help guide the consultant through the decision-making process for a school-based consultant: (a) Domains of Consultant Learning and Development, (b) Domains of Consultee Learning and Development, (c) Cultural Variations in the Consultation Constellation, (d) Contextual and Power Influences, and (e) Hypothesized Methods for Supporting Consultee and Client Success. By following this guided approach to multicultural school consultation, school-based consultants addressing the issue of bilingual education may be better able to (a) guide the conceptualization of the issues in the consultation process, (b) develop approaches for consulting within a cultural context, and (c) identify a variety of areas for future empirical investigation (Ingraham, 2000).

Rogers (2000), in a summary of major themes related to the cultural context of consultation, identified six cross-cultural competencies necessary for effective consultation. These cross-cultural competencies are discussed.

Understanding one's own and others' culture. This competency refers to the consultant's need to

> (a) examine his or her own cultural/ethnic/racial heritage and identity to be able to develop greater self-awareness of beliefs, prejudices, and assumptions; and (b) to learn about the cultural and sociopolitical background of the consultee and client to better understand and respect their perspectives, values, and histories with oppression. (Rogers, 2000, p. 416)

Developing cross-cultural communication and interpersonal skills. The consultant must develop the communication and interpersonal skills necessary to appropriately communicate the various bilingual education program options, the potential advantages and disadvantages of participation, and the rationale for recommendations in a way that is culturally and cross-culturally sensitive.

Examining the cultural embeddedness of consultation. Each step in the consultative process should be viewed through the framework of the cultural perspective of the consultee or client.

Using qualitative methodologies.   The consultant should possess the skills necessary to utilize single-subject design methodologies, naturalistic data-gathering techniques, and ethnographic and case study approaches to measure the effectiveness of bilingual education program participation and the related consultative process.

Acquiring culture-specific knowledge.   The consultant should have cultural-specific knowledge relevant for the particular consultee or client related to issues such as acculturation, immigration, parent's role in education, expected roles of teachers, and bilingual education services.

Understanding of and skill in working with interpreters.   This is an extremely important competency for school-based consultants and is often underdeveloped among practitioners. The limited number of culturally and linguistically diverse school personnel often necessitates extensive use of interpretation services. The interpreter often becomes the voice for the process, and skill in the selection and appropriate use of an interpreter is critical. Consultants should review the skills and competencies recommended for school-based interpreters (e.g., equally fluent in both languages, knowledgeable of school setting, trained in issues of confidentiality, etc.). Lopez (2000, 2002) provided an expanded discussion of this topic and issues related to the practice of using interpreters during instructional consultation activities (see Rhodes, 2000, for a practical guide for using interpreters in a school-based setting).

RECOGNITION OF THE EMOTIONALLY CHARGED NATURE OF THE DISCOURSE REGARDING BILINGUAL EDUCATION

The consultant's need for both a guided decision-making approach such as Ingraham's (2000) MSC framework and multicultural and cross-cultural competencies as described by Rogers (2000) is underscored by the emotionally charged nature of the discourse regarding bilingual education (see Benavides, 2002; Reyes, 2003). Few topics in education elicit such a visceral reaction among parents, educators, and administrators as bilingual education. Advanced recognition of this concern is fundamental to consultative endeavors. Because of the emotionally charged nature of the topic, the cultural, linguistic, and philosophical differences between the consultant and consultee or client are potentially magnified and may, if left unchecked, negatively influence the outcome of the consultative relationship.

It has been the authors' experience that the origin of an individual's view of bilingual education is varied and complex and is affected by their position and life experiences. As previously mentioned, parents of ELL students may often be hesitant to have their children placed in instructional settings that are anything other than English only. Many parents have endured the educational and emotional hardship that often accompanies limited English proficiency and earnestly desire their children to learn English as rapidly as possible. A viewpoint frequently expressed to the authors by parents is that they will assume responsibility for home-language maintenance if the school will assist in the development of English-language proficiency. However, this viewpoint cannot be generalized to all parents. On the other end of the continuum, numerous parents of ELL students are appreciative of the cultural and linguistic opportunities provided by bilingual education, are expectant that their children will be in environments that foster dual language development, and are unwilling to compromise the potential long-term academic gains that might be afforded through bilingual education (Shin, 2000).

Many teachers and administrators are also polarized in their opinion of bilingual education (Shin & Krashen, 1996). For the uninitiated, the idea of providing bilingual education (not to mention the need to learn about the various programs previously described) is a daunting task. This understandable apprehension and resistance may be intensified by a fear that as teachers or administrators they do not have the prerequisite cultural, linguistic, or academic knowledge to positively contribute to such a program. In addition to the administrative fear of heightened costs and teacher recruitment difficulties, it has been the authors' experience that it is also not uncommon for educators to question the need to cater to students and parents who "should be learning English anyway." This viewpoint seems to be most common among educators who have historically resisted bilingual education services for ELL students or who have only recently begun to serve an ELL population.

Knowledge of Court Rulings and Federal Law Related to Bilingual Education

Because of the controversial nature of the topic and the limited research and literature available to guide practice, it is important that individuals serving as consultants are well grounded in the legal aspects of bilingual education. The National Association for Bilingual Education (2001) provides a summary of federal law related to children who are ELL students. Students whose first language is other than English are considered language minorities and are given specific protection under federal law.

ELL students receive equal protection as afforded by the 14th Amendment of the U.S. Constitution and are protected under Title VI of the Civil Rights Act of 1964. Title VI prohibits discrimination in any federally funded activity on the basis of race, color, ethnicity, national origin, religion, or creed. *Lau v. Nichols* (1974) expanded the protection of ELL students and required all school districts to adequately serve limited English proficient students. Additional federal laws, such as Title III of the Elementary and Secondary Education Act of 2001, contain provisions to ensure the availability of funds for quality instructional programs for ELL students (National Association for Bilingual Education, 2001). The type and nature of programs will vary depending on whether there is a sufficient number of children to allow for such programs as specified by law.

Federal law also requires that all parents with children in federally funded bilingual education programs be notified as to why their children were selected for participation, be provided with alternatives to participation, and be given the option of declining to enroll their children in the program. Information must be presented to parents in a language they can understand.

It is imperative that school-based consultants accurately inform parents of the potential long-term consequences of not placing an ELL student in bilingual education (as delineated by the bilingual education effectiveness research previously discussed). Recommendations for bilingual education placement and participation should be based on information that is in accordance with federal and state law and on empirically validated data.

Knowledge of School-Specific Issues and Resources

School-based consultants addressing the area of bilingual education must also be familiar with school specific issues and resources. They should understand the types of programs that are currently available (e.g., pull-out ESL, content-based ESL, transitional bilingual programs, maintenance bilingual programs, or two-way or dual language bilingual education programs), the support these programs have historically received, the concerns they have generated, and the level of receptiveness to program alteration and development. Systemic issues such as a lack of qualified personnel, an absence of programmatic options, or stagnant program development may require the attention of a consultant before any individual student recommendations or solution-focused interventions can be successfully implemented.

Understanding of Student-Specific Skills and Needs

In addition to understanding the variety of programs available for ELL students and being able to advocate for change or improvement as necessary, school-based consultants must also have a clear understanding of student-specific skills and needs to work with parents and school personnel to select or create a program of choice. Examples of student-specific information that should be gathered or reviewed by the consultant are described.

Educational history.   Through record review and parent interview, the consultant should inquire about the country (or countries) in which the child has been educated, the language (or languages) of instruction, previous bilingual education services, reason for termination or exit from bilingual education services, grades repeated, number of schools attended, areas of academic success, and areas of academic difficulty or concern. If academic difficulties exist, it should be determined whether these difficulties are present across both languages or if they are manifest only when the student is required to perform academic tasks in English. If they are present only when the student is required to perform tasks in English, then this may be an indication of second language acquisition issues rather than a specific content knowledge deficit or disability.

Language history.   Through record review (e.g., home language surveys) and parent interviews, the language history of the child and family should be explored. What language or languages are currently used at home? What language or languages have been used at home during the life of the student? What language appears to be preferred by the student? In what language does the student prefer to read? In what language does the student watch TV or listen to music?

Current language proficiency.   The current language proficiency of the student should be examined through record review, teacher interview, and formal and informal assessment. The mere fact that a child appears to use one particular language more frequently should not serve as an indicator of language proficiency. The results of recently administered language proficiency measures provide insight into the student's level of language proficiency across both languages. The results should be no more than six months old and should be the product of a trained examiner using age and language appropriate measures. Both formal and informal procedures and tools are recommended to provide the broadest context possible for evaluating current language proficiency.

Second-language acquisition process. School-based consultants should be familiar with several seminal studies regarding the second-language acquisition process. Key sources of information include Cummins (1983, 1984), Ortiz and Polyzoi (1986), Collier (1987), and Thomas and Collier (1996, 1997, 2002). These and other studies provide critical information regarding the expected rate of second-language acquisition, the multiple factors that may influence language acquisition, the difference between basic communication and academic language skills, and the potential impact of second-language acquisition on academic achievement.

Understanding of Parent Specific Desires and Needs

When culturally and linguistically diverse parents are the recipients of consultative services, school-based consultants should initiate the process in accordance with the model of consultation selected (e.g., behavioral, ecological, instructional, mental health) while maintaining a focus on unique cultural, familial, and experiential perspectives of parents and students. As previously discussed, school-based consultants should develop an understanding of possible culture-specific communication styles, expected role of parents, expected role of school personnel, and the family's level of acculturation. Likewise, potential roadblocks to equitable parent participation when working with teachers and administrators (such as parents' English language skills) need to be fully understood and replaced with strategies leading to full parent participation (see National Institute on the Education of At-Risk Students, 1997). To better understand the possible cultural and social perspectives of parents, consultants should seek assistance from persons knowledgeable of the culture (i.e., cultural brokers), as necessary.

Understanding of Specific Skills and Needs of School Personnel

When school personnel are the recipients of consultative services, consultants should have an understanding of the consultee's role-specific skills and needs (e.g., regular education teacher, special education teacher, school administrator, etc.) to provide relevant and beneficial information and recommendations. Consultants should help school personnel gain an understanding of previously mentioned issues (e.g., bilingual education issues, court rulings and federal law, potential school-specific issues and resources, student-specific skills and needs, and parent-specific desires and needs) relevant to the specific situation that is targeted. School-based consultants should assist school personnel in working with students and parents to identify a program of choice, potential barriers to program participation, and necessary student-specific program adaptations. External support and training should be sought if additional information is needed regarding bilingual education program options, program implementation strategies, or legal considerations.

Evaluation of Program Effectiveness

Single-subject design methodologies, naturalistic data-gathering techniques, and ethnographic and case study approaches may be used by school-based consultants to measure the effectiveness of bilingual education programs and corresponding consultation activities. The consultation process with school personnel and culturally and linguistically diverse parents may be adjusted as needed. Likewise, information regarding the effectiveness of the bilingual education program structure and delivery and the participation decision-making process may be shared with interested consultees.

SUMMARY AND RECOMMENDATIONS FOR FUTURE RESEARCH

The actual application of the theories and strategies recommended in this article is often more difficult than anticipated. The intentional or unintentional political pressure generated within the school setting, the voiced and unvoiced expectations of parents of bilingual students, the comfort level and expertise of school personnel, and the limited existence of quality bilingual education programs are just a few of the potential barriers that school-based consultants may face when addressing this important issue.

To assist practitioners in moving from theoretical understanding to effective application, several important issues must be thoroughly understood by school-based consultants.

This article provides school-based consultants with an overview of the ELL student population, programs available to ELL students, research examining bilingual education programs, and guidelines and recommendations for the application of bilingual education knowledge to consultative practice with school personnel and culturally and linguistically diverse parents. Because of the paucity of research regarding school-based consultation related to bilingual education issues, guidelines and recommendations are presented within the larger framework of multicultural and cross-cultural consultation.

The authors strongly encourage future research in this area, particularly studies that examine effective consultation models for use with school personnel and culturally and linguistically diverse parents related to bilingual education. Research-based strategies that enhance the quality of school personnel and parent decision making related to program participation and methods for the evaluation of the consultative process and program effectiveness appear to be particularly important areas of inquiry.

REFERENCES

American Psychological Association. (2003). Guidelines on multicultural education, training, research, practice and organizational change for psychologists. *American Psychologist 58,* 377–402.

Antunez, B., & Zelasko, N. (2001). *What program models exist to serve English language learners?* Retrieved July 23, 2003, from http:www.ncela.gwu/askncela/22models.htm

August, D., & Hakuta, K. (1998). *Educating language-minority children.* Washington, DC: National Academy Press.

Baca, L. (2004). Bilingualism and bilingual education. In L. M. Baca. & H. Cervantes (Eds.), *The bilingual special education interface* (pp. 24–45). Columbus, OH: Pearson Prentice Hall.

Baker, K., & de Kanter, A. A. (1981). *Effectiveness of bilingual education: A review of the literature.* Washington, DC: U.S. Department of Education, Office of Planning, Budget, & Evaluation.

Baker, K., & de Kanter A. A. (1983). Federal policy and the effectiveness of bilingual education. In K. Baker & A. de Kanter (Eds.), *Bilingual education: A reappraisal of federal policy* (pp. 33–86). Lexington, MA: Lexington.

Benavides, A. H. (2002). Bilingual education: A dream unfulfilled. *Bilingual Research Journal, 26,* v–xi.

Borg, W. (1987). *Applying educational research: A practical guide for teachers* (2nd ed.). New York: Longman.

Brisk, M. E. (1998). *Bilingual education: From compensatory to quality schooling.* Mahwah, NJ: Lawrence Erlbaum Associates, Inc.

Borg, W., & Gall, M. D. (1989). *Educational research: An introduction* (5th ed.). New York: Longman.

Civil Rights Act of 1963 (Public Law 88–352) 42 U.S.C. 2000d.

Collier, V. (1987). Age and rate of acquisition of second language for academic purposes. *TESOL Quarterly, 21,* 617–641.

Crawford, J. (1999). *Bilingual education: History, politics, theory and practice* (4th ed.). Los Angeles: Bilingual Educational Services.

Cummins, J. (1983). Bilingualism and special education: Program and pedagogical issues. *Learning Disability Quarterly, 6,* 373–386.

Cummins, J. (1984). *Bilingual special education issues in assessment and pedagogy.* San Diego, CA: College-Hill.

Elementary and Secondary Education Act, The No Child Left Behind Education Act of 2001. (Public Law 107–110) 20 U.S.C. 6301.

Feinberg, R.C. (2002). *Bilingual education: A reference handbook.* Santa Barbara, CA: ABC-CLIO.

Greene, J. P. (1998). *A meta-analysis of the effectiveness of bilingual education.* Retrieved November 11, 2002, from http:www.ourworld.compuserve.com/homepages/jcrawford.greene.htm

Hernandez, D. J., & Darke, K. (1999). Socioeconomic and demographic risk factors and resources among children in immigrants and native-born families: 1910, 1960, and 1990. In D. J. Hernandez (Ed.), *Children of immigrants: Health, adjustment and public assistance* (pp. 19–125). Washington, DC: National Academy Press.

Ingraham, C. L. (2000). Consultation through a multicultural lens: Multicultural and cross-cultural consultation in schools. *School Psychology Review, 29,* 320–343.

Kindler, A. L. (2002). *Survey of the states' limited English proficient students and available educational programs and services 1999–2000 summary report.* Washington, DC: National Clearinghouse for English Acquisition and Language Instruction Educational Programs.

Lau v. Nichols, 414 U.S. 563 (1974).

Liu, H., & Fern, V. (2003). *How does the shortage of language proficient personnel affect U.S. interests?* Retrieved July 23, 2003, from http:www.ncela.gwu.edu/askncela/15impact.htm

Lopez, E. C. (2000). Conducting instructional consultation through interpreters. *School Psychology Review, 29,* 378–388.

Lopez, E. C. (2002). Best practices in working with school interpreters to deliver psychological services to children and families. *Best practices in school psychology* (4th ed., pp.1419–1432). Washington, DC: National Association of School Psychologists.

National Association for Bilingual Education. (2001). *What does federal law say regarding services for LEP students?* Retrieved September 25, 2003, from http:www.nabe.org.faq_detail.asp?ID=16

National Center for Educational Statistics. (1997). *The condition of education 1997, supplemental table 4–1.* Retrieved September 3, 2002, from http:nces.ed.gov.pubs/ce/c97040d01.html.

National Center for Educational Statistics. (2002). *Schools and staffing survey, 1999–2000: Overview of the data for public, private, charter, and bureau of Indian affairs elementary and secondary schools* (NCES 2002–313). Washington, DC: Author.

National Clearinghouse for English Language Acquisition and Language Instruction Educational Programs. (1996). *Why is it important to maintain the native language?* Retrieved July 23, 2003, from http:www.ncela.gwu.askncela/12native.html

National Clearinghouse for English Language Acquisition and Language Instruction Educational Programs. (2002a). *United States most commonly spoken languages.* Retrieved August 13, 2002, from http:www.ncbe.gwu.edu/askncela/05toplangs.html

National Clearinghouse for English Language Acquisition and Language Instruction Educational Programs. (2002b). *United States rate of LEP growth*. Retrieved August 13, 2002, from http:www.ncbe.gwu.edu/states/stateposter.pdf

National Institute on the Education of At-Risk Students. (1997). *Overcoming barriers to family involvement in Title I schools: Report to Congress.* Washington, DC: Policy Studies Associates.

O'Malley, J. (1978). Review of the evaluation of the impact of ESEA Title VII Spanish/English bilingual education programs. *Bilingual Resources, 1,* 6–10.

Ortiz, A. A., & Polyzoi, E. (1986). *Characteristics of limited English proficient Hispanic students in programs for the learning disabled: Implications for policy, practice and research. Part I. Report summary* (ERIC Document Reproduction Service No. ED 267 578) Austin, TX.

Ovando, C. J., & Collier, V. P. (1998). *Bilingual and ESL classrooms: Teaching in cultural contexts* (2nd ed.). Boston: McGraw-Hill.

Porter, R. P. (1998). *The case against bilingual education* (Reprinted from *The Atlantic Monthly*). Retrieved July 11, 2003, from http:www.ceousa.org/READ/porter1.html

Ramirez, J. D., Yuen, S. D., & Ramey, D. R. (1991). *Final report: Longitudinal study of structured English immersion strategy, early-exit and late-exit transitional bilingual programs for language-minority children: Executive summary.* San Mateo, CA: Aguirre International.

Reyes, L. O. (2003). Surviving the "perfect storm": Bilingual education policymaking in New York City. *Journal of Latinos and Education, 2,* 23–30.

Rhodes, R. L. (2000). Legal and professional issues in the use of interpreters: A fact sheet for school psychologists. *National Association of School Psychologists Communiqué, 29,* 28.

Rogers, M. R. (2000). Examining the cultural context of consultation. *School Psychology Review, 29,* 414–418.

Roseberry-McKibbin, C. (2002). *Multicultural students with special language needs: Practical strategies for assessment and intervention* (2nd ed.), Oceanside, CA: Academic Communications.

Rossell, C. H., & Baker, K. (1996). The educational effectiveness of bilingual education. *Research in the Teaching of English, 30,* 7–74.

Shin, F. H. (2000). Parent attitudes toward the principles of bilingual education and their children's participation in bilingual education. *Journal of Intercultural Studies, 21,* 93–100.

Shin, F. H., & Krashen, S. (1996). Teacher attitude toward the principles of bilingual education and toward student's participation in bilingual programs: Same or different? *Bilingual Research Journal, 20,* 45–54.

Tarver Behring, S., & Ingraham, C. L. (1998). Culture as a central component to consultation: A call to the field. *Journal of Educational & Psychological Consultation, 9,* 57–72.

Thomas, W., & Collier, V. (1996). *Language minority student achievement and program effectiveness.* Fairfax, VA: George Mason University, Center for Bilingual/Multicultural/ESL Education.

Thomas, W. P., & Collier, V. (1997). *School effectiveness for language minority students.* Washington, DC: National Clearinghouse for Bilingual Education.

Thomas, W. P., & Collier, V. P. (2002). A national study of school effectiveness for language minority students' long-term academic achievement: Retrieved September 4, 2002, from http:www.crede.uscu.edu/research/llaa1.html

U.S. Census Bureau. (2001). *Percent of persons who are foreign born: 2000.* Washington, DC: Author.

Weaver, L., & Padron Y. (1999). Language of instruction and its impact on educational access and outcomes. In A. Tashakkori & S. H. Ochoa (Eds.), *Reading on equal education: Volume 16 education of Hispanics in the United States: Politics, policies and outcomes* (pp. 75–92). New York: AMS Press.

Willig, A. (1985). A meta-analysis of selected studies on the effectiveness of bilingual education. *Review of Educational Research, 55,* 269–317.

Zappert. L., & Cruz, B. (1977). *Bilingual education: An appraisal of empirical research.* Berkeley, CA: Bay Area Bilingual Education League.

Salvador Hector Ochoa, PhD, is an Associate Professor at Texas A&M University where he has a joint appointment in the school psychology and special education programs. Dr. Ochoa is the Associate Editor of the *American Educational Research Journal: Teaching, Learning and Human Development.* His research focuses on educational programming and psychoeducational assessment issues pertaining to Hispanic English Language Learner students

Robert L. Rhodes, PhD, NCSP, is Department Chair for New Mexico State University's Special Education/Communication Disorders Department, and is a school psychology faculty member. He has served as President of the New Mexico Association of School Psychologists, State Delegate to the National Association of School Psychologists, and is an Associate Editor of the *School Psychology Quarterly* journal for Division 16 of the American Psychological Association. Dr. Rhodes's research has focused on intervention strategies for culturally and linguistically diverse students and neuropsychological applications in the schools.

JOURNAL OF EDUCATIONAL AND PSYCHOLOGICAL CONSULTATION, *16*(1&2), 95–111
Copyright © 2005, Lawrence Erlbaum Associates, Inc.

Toma el Tiempo:[1]
The Wisdom of Migrant Families in Consultation

Mary M. Clare
Lewis & Clark College

Anna Jimenez and Jennifer McClendon
Oregon Health & Science University

Children of migrant farm working families often live and learn in conditions that conspire against both health and education. At the same time, these children are as capable as any in our nation. Education and health care professionals are frequently in positions to support these capabilities and migrant families can be significant contributors to the success of education and health programs. However, the variables obstructing collaboration with migrant families are numerous and often go unidentified. More invisible are the variables supporting natural and positive inclusion of these families in problem-solving processes. This article reveals both barriers and avenues to connecting with migrant farm working families so their children may gain greater benefits from health and educational services.

In the rally in Palm Springs, more than 300 immigrants, parishioners and union members joined the bus riders at Our Lady of Solitude Church. The signs said "Immigrants are today's slaves" and "I cut your grass, I make your bed, I wash your dishes, I pick your fruit. I refuse to be invisible." (Greenhouse, 2003)

Correspondence should be sent to Mary M. Clare, Lewis & Clark College, 615 S. W. Palatine Hill Rd., MSC 86, CPSY, Portland, OR 97219. E-mail: clare@1clark.edu.
[1]Take the time.

The meal you had last night was brought to you, in some part, by people who are migrant farm workers. Most of the seasonal vegetables and fruits offered in our grocery stores are harvested by the poorest and least welcomed members of the United States' populace. Most of these laborers are Mexican people who have chosen this work out of desperation when conditions in their home country make leaving to find work the only viable chance for survival (Davis, 1990; Ruiz-de-Velasco & Fix, 2000).

Ten years ago, 80% of the Mexican people filling these roles were in the United States legally (Fix & Passel, 1994). Now, only 50% enjoy this security due to shifts in immigration policy that have made documentation as a visiting worker increasingly difficult to secure (U.S. Department of Labor, 2000). The median age of migrant farm laborers is 30 with 67% of those workers being under 35 and 20% being women (U.S. Department of Labor, 2000). Available demographics indicate that most migrant farm laborers have children (Ruiz-de-Velasco & Fix, 2000). These children are legally protected in their civil rights to have access to free and public education (Pyler v. Doe, 1982), and, within limits, to public health care (Keppel, 2000).

This year, it appears the possibility of legal status may be extended again to the more than 8 million immigrant laborers who consistently work in the migrant stream (Bazar, 2004; Pulaski, 2003). Under the currently proposed federal plan, legal status will not be immediate, and in many cases will only be temporary. Green cards allowing time-limited residence and employment in the United States may be provided to many of these workers and some provisions of the plan allow for naturalization of laborers after continuous engagement in the U.S. workforce for a number of years. For qualifying families, this policy change may relieve some of the stress associated with documentation. However, the oppression of migrant farm workers is not sustained by public policy alone. The extent to which any policy of inclusion is translated into positive change in the experiences of migrant people is dependent in large part on the related practices of individual health care and education professionals.

One way service providers can act to demonstrate inclusion and respect for migrant farm working people is by establishing collaborative consultation relationships with migrant families to address the health and education needs of their children (Henning-Stout, 1996; Huang & Gibbs, 1992; Lopez, Scribner, & Mahitivanichcha, 2001; Shi & Singh, 1998). There are numerous obstacles to this collaboration, not the least of which is the lack of established practice for developing such relationships (Martinez & Velazquez, 2001). Other obstructions arise from socially sustained systems of oppression that perpetuate the marginal status of migrant people by retaining practices that exclude or ignore their concerns and interests. The consequent invisibility of this population prevents acknowledgement and engagement of the assets migrant families have for supporting their children's health and education.

Later, we offer particular consideration of obstructions and assets relevant to consultation with migrant families in the context of both broad social conditions and particular familial or cultural variables. In the case of people on the migrant stream, health considerations are inseparable from challenges these people face related to education and mental health. The health disparity among ethnic groups is well established, with Latino migrant farm workers among the most vulnerable to health concerns while also receiving the least care (Keppel, 2000). Children of migrant families are also vulnerable to dropping out of the educational system and having frequently interrupted school attendance due to the nature of families' living conditions (Lopez et al., 2001). The consultant in health care and education will often have information of use to one another. Whether this information increases access or provides insight into ways of best serving migrant families and children, a conversation between these two areas of consultation seems warranted and serves as the basis of this article.

Drawing on contemporary theory in public health, we structure our discussion around the notion of access. Shi and Singh (1998, p. 465) defined access to care as "timely use of needed, affordable, convenient, acceptable, and effective" service. We first consider the typical circumstances of migrant life as they mitigate against access to health care and education. Next we apply considerations of access to the practice of consultation in both fields to demonstrate ways of tapping the strength and wisdom of these families as collaborators in support of their children's education and health so the benefits children and families receive in both areas may be substantially increased.

LIFE CIRCUMSTANCES AND ACCESS
TO PUBLIC SERVICE

"The vast majority of these people are working, and many of them face unscrupulous employers who take advantage of them," said Antonio Villaraigosa, a Los Angeles City Council member and former mayoral candidate. "We need a humane, sensible immigration policy that takes into account that these people have worked here for years, they pay taxes, their children are living here." (Greenhouse, 2003)

Issues of poverty, particularities of family structure, language, and cultural values such as the centrality of family, deference to authority, fatalism, and spiritual tradition are all practical considerations with immediate relevance to the access migrant farm working families have to education and health care services. In addition to these circumstances, the conditions in which migrant families live and work have significant bearing on access.

Migrant farm working families are poor. They live in a poverty most of the people reading this article can hardly imagine, so distant are these conditions from our own. Poverty reduces options in all areas of life (Lott, 2001). For these families, there are fewer options for healthy eating, for health care, and for success in any of the existing social systems (e.g., public education, public health, community prevention services). Migrancy compounds these challenges and is seen in differences in health risk patterns when migrant people are compared with people who do not migrate (Marmot, 1999). Cultural bereavement may also be central to the experience of these families who have left their homeland in desperate search for means of family survival and entered a culture that is both unfamiliar and often hostile to their presence (Helman, 1994).

Mexican families, representing the vast majority of families reliant on migrant farm work for their livelihood, can contain 3 to 400 or more people. The average size of these families is likely somewhere closer to the larger number (Suarez-Orozco & Suarez-Orozco, 2001). Large segments of these families tend to migrate together, or, as word travels back to family in Mexico, to establish themselves in the same rural U.S. communities (Gamboa & Buan, 1995). Thus, individuals and families are less likely to seek help from a health care or educational professional, but will turn instead to extended family and community.

Children are integral, everyday parts of migrant culture and not restricted by dominant-culture adult norms of being more quiet and sedate in mixed-age situations. Younger families often live with the husband's family of origin making the parental grandparents integral to family identity and function (Suarez-Orozco & Suarez-Orozco, 2001). Thus, the dominant culture understanding of supporting children by engaging their parents must be adapted to the circumstances of migrant children who are parented by many family members (including siblings, grandparents, aunts, uncles, and close family friends or *compadres*).

Migrant families are tended most closely by the women, who usually do not drive and have both limited access to mass transit and limited finances to afford bus or train fare (Martinez & Velazquez, 2001). At the same time, mothers tend not to make decisions without conferring with fathers, particularly around private issues (e.g., birth control). Thus, evidence of *ma-*

chismo (the man's role as provider and agent in the public world) and *marianismo* (the woman's role as nurturer and agent in the domestic and spiritual world) are common and in force in many migrant families (Falicov, 1998).

Language is often a limiting factor for migrant families' interactions with education and health care systems (Merino, Trueba, & Samaniego, 1993). Migrant parents may speak neither Spanish nor English, but a blend of the two languages or an indigenous language (Henning-Stout, 1996; Merino et al., 1993). Even when language appears not to be a concern, words often carry variable meaning across cultures, particularly when one speaker is from a culture emphasizing verbal content and the other is from a culture emphasizing nonverbal content (Hall, 1976; Sue & Sue, 2003).

Mexican culture often conveys to children a strong respect for figures of authority (La Roche & Shirberg, 2004). This deference to authority, or *respeto,* then continues into adulthood. For example, in deference to authority, both students and adults will avoid eye contact and will refrain from questioning others. Many families and students have reported educators and health care providers meeting this deference with attributions of passivity, lack of interest, or resistance to the services offered (La Roche & Shirberg, 2004).

The common knowledge held by migrant workers, that is, knowledge collected by living and moving through life, is not necessarily compatible with contemporary educational and medical practices and understandings of learning and health. Many of these families have strong indigenous backgrounds and embrace value systems steeped in traditional culture with regard to learning and healing. Public health scholars suggest that it is incumbent on service providers to use the family's belief system to make them well (Shi & Singh, 1998). For example, if Mexican parents suspect evil spirits or *sustos,* they will respond best to the presence and collaboration of a *curandera/o* (traditional folk healer) in the healing process (Gamboa & Buan, 1995).

Closely linked with orientations toward learning and healing is the tendency of Mexican migrants to relate to life problems from a position often described as fatalism (Magana & Hovey, 2003). Fatalism in this culture is characterized by peaceful acceptance of what is and may be understood as the opposite of the opportunism characteristic of the dominant culture. Mexican migrant families are likely to live from themes of "We'll make do," "It's okay like this," but will at the same time sacrifice anything for their children's well-being. Numerous families have complained to the authors that their seemingly passive orientation to problems is too often interpreted by schools as indicating that the families do not care.

Compounding the deference to authority is the sense that many families have of imminent deportation. Currently, more than 8 million migrant people in the United States are undocumented (Bazar, 2004). For families, the threat of deportation prevents their advocating for themselves or their children in educational and health care settings. Our experience has shown that families simply will not seek services if they have any sense that they will be required to produce a social security number or if they have any suspicion of links between service agencies and the Immigration and Naturalization Service. As we have observed this phenomenon repeatedly, we have come also to understand the strength, complexity, and activity of the communication network (word of mouth) among migrant farm workers. Earning the trust of migrant people has been an absolute prerequisite to our providing any consultation services related to education or health care.

Finally, workplace and housing conditions stand as daily obstructions to healthy living for migrant families (Magana & Hovey, 2003). Although public advocacy for migrant farm workers on the part of local and national organizations has brought the situations faced by these families to greater general awareness, the conditions seem not to improve. Limitations in work safety related to exposure to toxins (e.g., with pesticides), increased incidence of work-related accidents, extreme weather conditions, extended work hours, pay-by-weight policies that interfere with taking breaks, and greatly limited sanitary facilities contribute significantly to the health needs of this population while restricting time and attention for considering educational and health care concerns or interests.

Each of the realities mentioned here is generally understood as an obstruction or barrier to full participation by migrant families in public services. To complete the picture of life circumstances encountered by these families, issues of equity in access to education and health care must also be considered. Most immediately, this access is evident in families' lack of familiarity with and related inability to navigate education and health systems. The strangeness of the systems migrant families encounter in the United States is compounded by poverty and differences in culture and language, but is also sustained by policies and practices within public service organizations.

In the next section of this article, we offer suggestions for engaging migrant families in consultation based in alternative interpretations of many of these circumstances. Our suggestions support basing consultation in the assets migrant families bring to relationships in schools and health care clinics.

FAMILY ASSETS AND CONSULTATION

"I think the people in the United States are fair minded," said Dolores Huerta, a rider who founded the United Farm Workers with Cesar Chavez. "When you have people who are being oppressed, who are not being paid fairly, whose children suffer, this is not fair, and we have to change that." (Greenhouse, 2003)

The importance of addressing the concerns and interests of Mexican immigrants in general, and migrant farm workers specifically, has been initially established in consultation-related literature (Bursztyn, 2002; Henning-Stout, 1996). However, knowing of the existence of need does not guarantee responding effectively and respectfully to that need. As Hall (1997) warned psychologists, it is vital that we take humble and ruthless stock of our practices to note obsolescence in the face of expanding presence and awareness of people from diverse life circumstances.

The idea of access is immediately applicable in assessments of the responsiveness or obsolence of consultation. Practical circumstances, such as those described earlier, define the daily lives of migrant farm workers and stand as barriers to the engagement of migrant families on behalf of their children in education and health care settings. Hidden in some of these circumstances are characteristics of wisdom and strength that may be acknowledged and empowered by service providers to reduce these barriers and enhance the relevance and responsiveness of the services available to migrant farm working families.

Family

Probably the most profound asset brought by Mexican migrant families to the occasion of consultation is the strength of allegience to the family (Ramos, 2003; Valencia & Black, 2002). Like all parents, migrant parents want what is best for their children. In life choices and in their narrative descriptions, these parents have been found consistently to demonstrate their devotion by giving all they have in support of these best interests (Ramos, 2003). It is the task of education and health care service providers to relate to this profound strength rather than to the historically prevalent deficit story that has pervaded dominant culture lore with regard to Mexican migrant families (Valencia & Black, 2002).

Migrant families function within the demands of their life situations. Within these constraints, they interact with schools and health care professionals. In research demonstrating methods for engaging families in support of Latino children's reading skill development, Arzubiaga, Rueda, and Monzo (2002) observed ways of shifting curricula to have a better fit with the daily realities of Latino learners. This study of ecocultural factors mediating children's opportunities to engage in reading activities can be taken as an opportunity to see and address the obsolecence of educational practices for Latino children. The specific findings of this study supported the identification of three ecocultural factors linked with reading motivation: culture and language, nurturance, and domestic workload.

Related to culture and language, Arzubiaga et al.,'s (2002) study indicated that migrant children had more success with reading when their family involved them in literacy activities related to the family's religious practices. This combination of reading activity with culturally congruent context significantly correlated with learners' self-concepts as readers and with progress in the development of reading skills.

A second factor, nurturance, was indicated by the time a family spent together and the extent of the family's promotion of family values and identity. Nurturance was positively correlated with children's reading development and self-concepts as readers. Among the authors' conclusions related to the importance of nurturance in these families is the warning that family systems perspectives will only be useful for identifying best interventions with migrant children if primary consideration is given to the daily realities of family life that require significant participation by the children in survival routines.

Consistent with this insight, the study revealed a third factor in the family's domestic workload showing this work demand to be inversely proportional to children's value on reading. Migrant families living in poverty must give more time and effort to family survival and children are expected to contribute to meeting domestic workload demands (e.g., child care, food preparation). Arzubiaga et al. (2002) suggested that a legitimate effort toward engaging migrant families in consultation includes developing and implementing policies that lighten the family's workload burden (such as subsidized child care in schools and clinics or financial assistance for domestic appliances that give family members more time to engage in supporting learning and health).

An additional and related consideration for migrant families is transportation. Having clinics at any distance from the community or serving only one person at a time (i.e., the individual child separate from his or her family) is, for this cultural group, not only obsolete (Hall, 1997), but has always been a significant access issue limiting the use and relevance of educational (Suarez-Orozco & Suarez-Orozco, 2001) and health services (Marmot, 1999).

Specific programs for addressing both the issues of domestic workload and transportation are found in programs linked with school nursing, with public health care clinics, and with education (see Nuestra Comunidad Sana, 2004). Most of these programs are based in community action and organization and remain without description in the literature (Putnam & Feldstein, 2003). Along the Columbia River in Washington and Oregon, a public health program involves both school and public health nurses in recruiting and supporting *promatoras*, migrant community members who serve as family advocates with regard to health care issues. Promatoras speak with families about the effectiveness of Western medicine in ways that facilitate access by building trust (J. Hernandez, personal communication, January 23, 2004).

Similar programs in education recognize the importance of building relationships with families through community-based family advocates (Putnam & Feldstein, 2003). In these cases, educators and educational paraprofessionals link with migrant community members who can serve as liaisons with families, a role that is far more than language translation because of its involvement in translating one culture to another. In Wenatchee, Washington, teachers understood that they were not communicating well with migrant parents and initiated programs to engage and learn from the families (J. Hernandez, personal communication, January 23, 2004). Initial focus groups revealed that the parents themselves were intimidated by school situations because of their limited English, concern about schools' links with *La Migra* (immigration officials), and confusion about how schools function (with particular concern about homework). In response to these concerns, the district brought in a series of experts to familiarize school personnel with Latino culture. This led to the recruitment of migrant home visitors; bilingual and usually bicultural personnel who would go to family homes to discuss, in Spanish, teacher's concerns regarding children's academic progress. The home visitors would also assess the family's needs and concerns. Often, the home visitors found the educational issues to be among many issues and would serve to link families with public health and other public assistance programs.

In both health care and education, effective service rests on a deep understanding of migrant families. Successful programs understand the mother as the primary caregiver in the family. In matters of health, she is the repository of information passed down from mother to daughter and decides when an illness is beyond her ability to treat. At that point, she will seek help from family members, community healers like *curanderas* (or *curanderos*), and Western medicine (Mikhail, 1994).

The asset for these families is their proven ability to survive and the centrality of the collective—the family—to that survival. For migrant farm workers and their children, the family is the reliable center of the practical and spiritual life experience. Deference to this value must be at the center of any attempt by educators and health care service providers to plan for supporting migrant children. Each of the considerations mentioned earlier—daily routine for family survival, family workload, and transportation—can be understood as variables (neither barriers nor assets) at play in consultation. The family does not have options in any of these areas unless demands are lessened from without.

In the initial stages of consultation, when the learning or health issues a child is facing are being identified (Gutkin & Curtis, 1999) and when the family's wisdom and agency are being sought (Huang & Gibbs, 1992), consultants may respond to the realities of migrant family life by adjusting service to fit in the family routine. Consultants who bring resources to bear on reducing a family's workload and travel to the family home to eliminate the necessity of transportation are more likely to engage the family and support the child. Although seemingly time consuming, the long-term gain from building family-school teams with migrant families will likely be reflected in a learner's educational advancement and health status and in a reduced need for subsequent service (Lopez et al., 2001).

Language

The collaborative problem solving that is possible within the relational container of consultation is greatly enhanced when the language used by the participants is similar (Rogers, 1998). More often than not, the language of migrant families will be other than that of the dominant culture of schools and health care agencies (sometimes an indigenous language). The presence of bilingual service providers can be of great help, and it appears that, in general, migrant families feel more comfortable with Latino service providers regardless of the language match (Magana & Hovey, 2003; Zoucha, 1998). This preference likely has to do with the greater importance of cultural match for these families who are most often met with confusion, disrespect, or some other expression of misunderstanding that discounts and finally inhibits their attempts to interact with public culture.

In a study with parents of migrant preschoolers, Henning-Stout (1995) found that parents are interested in their children retaining their native language and culture while becoming proficient in English and learning how to function in the dominant culture of the United States. These desires represent assets brought by migrant families in that bilingualism and biculturalism are linked with higher levels of cognitive functioning, particularly when children have learned basic skills in their original language (i.e., fluency in reading, writing, speaking, and numeric reasoning) while building proficiency with English (Thomas & Collier, 1997). Migrant families also bring an orientation toward authority that supports entry into consultation. We discuss this characteristic in more detail later, but mention it here because of the evidence that even the interjection of minimal Spanish into the interaction can build trust and enhance the engagement of families in consultation (Magana & Hovey, 2003; Zoucha, 1998).

Culture

Mexican migrant people, like all people, are most comfortable in their own culture. Not only is migrant culture one that draws on the heritage and traditions of Mexico (Arredondo, 2002), it is also a culture defined in significant ways by poverty and by migrancy (Marmot, 1999). The circumstances of migrant life present clear challenges when it comes to ensuring that the educational and health care needs of children are being met. At the same time, the culture of Mexican migrant families can be dignified and engaged as assets for consultation in support of their children.

Machismo and marianismo. These two terms are understood differently by people of the culture and outside of the culture in which they originated. In the case of Mexican migrant farm working families, the presence of the complex of behaviors and beliefs associated with *machismo* and *marianismo* may be potential points of engagement for consultation (Arredondo, 2002; Stevens, 1998). At the same time, it is vital to see all people simultaneously as individuals, group members, and as people sharing universal traits; so that interpretation of these two constructs must be subject to that multiple perception (Bracero, 1998; Torres, Solberg, & Carlstrom, 2002).

In many migrant families, machismo is evident in the adult men's sense of obligation and related behaviors toward providing for the well-being of the family (Torres et al., 2002). Machismo implies the role of navigating the public world on behalf of the family (Stevens, 1998). Although this value can be expressed in ways that are oppressive to women in both intimate and public relationships (e.g., including psychotherapy; Bracero, 1998), its larger application is to the family's health and safety. Because their primary role is one of ensuring that the family has resources to survive, men may not appear active in consultation situations. However, fathers and other men in the family may be recruited to more active roles as resources for providing materials needed for the education or health of their children. The men of migrant families may therefore see more of the world's realities and be persuaded toward active support of children's education and health care as ways of ensuring children's success as they enter that world.

Consistent with the cultural construct of marianismo, adult women in migrant families may tend to focus on nurturing the family so that work and survival are possible (Arredondo, 2002; Stevens, 1998). Mothers and other women in the family naturally wish the best for their children within the frame of the demands of family life. Migrant women may be drawn to consultation when the importance of their involvement is clearly linked with children's health and well-being. In addition and as mentioned earlier, any reduction in the demands on the family can increase the time women have for being actively involved in children's interaction with education and health care programs (Arzubiaga et al., 2002).

Respeto.   Migrant families bring to consultation the asset of respect for and readiness to comply with perceived authority (La Roche & Shirberg, 2004). This compliance may be cursory if the content of discussions and plans in consultation do not fit with the realities of the family's life. Family survival is the primary necessity and focus of these families and will supersede any activity that is not deemed essential to that objective. Cursory evidence of *respeto* will appear in seeming agreement with suggestions made by consultants followed by no indication of the family's taking action on those suggestions.

Respeto can, however, be a key factor in the full engagement of migrant families in consultation on educational and health care matters related to their children. Once family members understand their role in a child's well-being and survival, strong and active involvement on the part of the family will likely result out of respect for authority in service to the child and family's well-being. This commitment can be retained and fortified by consultants taking time with the family. Taking time to establish a relationship—to get to know the family (Lopez et al., 2001)—is also central to the etiquette most recognized and honored by most Mexican families (Zoucha, 1998). Respeto can allow for the consultant to join with the family for understanding their interpretation of a child's learning or health problem. With respeto established and the realities of migrant family life understood, it is likely that the family's engagement at all points in consultation will be greatly enhanced.

Traditional and spiritual ways. Many migrant families maintain traditional understandings of illness and other misfortunes (Avila & Parker, 1999). Although orientations such as *fatalismo* (the idea that negative conditions cannot be avoided and are God's will) and ideas of cause such as *susto* (illness or other malfunctioning due to a traumatic or frightening experience) may strike consultants of the dominant culture as unusual, the deep commitment to these understandings on the part of migrant families can be used as resources for consultation. For example, supporting the family in seeking traditional healing or *curanderismo* can increase the family's readiness to become engaged in other ways of supporting children's education and health.

A particularly useful technique for engaging families in clarifying the nature and content of their concerns is to invite storytelling. In a study with recent Mexican immigrants, Bracero (1998) found that participants were more inclined to attend group therapy and follow through with therapeutic suggestions when they were supported in narrative descriptions of their experiences. Two possibilities for consultation seem to follow from these findings. First, engaging migrant families in storytelling may significantly increase their participation in consultation. Second, working with groups of families may enhance the quality of problem identification and intervention development and implementation.

DIRECTIONS FOR FUTURE PRACTICE AND RESEARCH

Largely because migrant families have such limited access to educational and health services, current practitioners and scholars in these disciplines know almost nothing about these families' needs, interests, and capabilities relative to supporting the education and health of their children. Although the growing literature on the experiences and interests of Latinos relative to education and health care can be of some help in understanding migrant families, there is strong evidence that migrancy shifts risk patterns (Marmot, 1999). Research specific to risks to learning and health for migrant children is greatly needed. In addition, each of the areas of asset described earlier ought to be further explored in practice with related consultation strategies made more generally available through practice-based research and publication.

Our experiences as consultants with migrant families demonstrate consistently that issues of health are immediately relevant to educational success, and access to education supports knowledge necessary for understanding health and health care. We are not advocating that all consultants in either field become accomplished in the other, but rather that we draw from one another's understandings about working with migrant families and remain prepared to collaborate across our professions.

In both health care and education, consultants may better serve migrant families by (a) slowing down to establish relationships with the families as a part of the consultation process, (b) drawing on the strengths of these families and their culture, (c) recognizing the necessity of attending to issues of domestic workload as central to consultation toward any useful intervention, and (d) using our own access within prevailing social service and governmental systems to challenge and revise policies and practices that conspire against migrant families having access to public education and health care.

Too little research and theory development is available to educators and health care providers for guiding our work with this population. Particular initiatives might include measuring the effect on consultation of consultant access to state programs that provide record-keeping technologies for school districts and health clinics serving migrant children and families. Of greatest use would be investigation of the impact relationship building with migrant families has as a part of consultation. In this context, the effect of consultants' engagement with issues of greatest concern to migrant families as they relate to the learning or health of children could be measured. The facilitation of contact with migrant families by making home visits, connecting families with workload reducing services (e.g., child care), and supporting the engagement of families in cultural activities that involve related academic skill development in their children (e.g., reading in religious settings) are just three possible areas of investigation that can provide insight into culturally respectful ways of entering into useful consultation relationships. Breaking from the tendency to view migrant children and families in terms of deficits and focusing instead on further articulation of assets inherent in the cultural and social mores of Mexican and Latino migrant families seems an important next step for guiding responsive consultation.

REFERENCES

Arredondo, P. (2002). Mujeres Latinas: Santas y marquesas. *Cultural Diversity and Ethnic Minority Psychology, 8,* 308–319.

Arzubiaga, A., Rueda, R., & Monzo, L. (2002). Family matters related to the reading engagement of Latino children. *Journal of Latinos and Education, 1,* 231–243.

Avila, E., & Parker, J. (1999). *Woman who glows in the dark: A curandera reveals traditional aztec secrets of physical and spiritual health.* New York: Tarcher/Putnam.

Bazar, E. (2004, January 8). Critics fear ripple effects of Bush immigration proposal. *Sacramento Bee.* Retrieved January 29, 2004, from http://www.sacbee.com/content/politics/story/8062550p-8995313c.html

Bracero, W. (1998). Intimidades, confianza, gender and hierarchy in the construction of Latino–Latina therapeutic relationships. *Cultural Diversity and Mental Health, 4,* 264–277.

Bursztyn, A. (2002). The path to academic disability: Javier's school experience. In C. Korn & A. Bursztyn (Eds.), *Rethinking multicultural education: Case studies in cultural transition* (pp. 160–184). Westport, CT: Bergin & Garvey.

Davis, M. P. (1990). *Mexican voices/American dreams.* New York: Holt.

Falicov, C. J. (1998). *Latino families in therapy: A guide to multicultural practice.* New York: Guilford.

Fix, M., & Passel, J. S. (1994). *Immigration and immigrants: Setting the record straight.* Washington, DC: The Urban Institute.

Gamboa, E., & Buan, C. (1995). *Nosotros: The Hispanic people of Oregon.* Portland, OR: Oregon Council for the Humanities.

Greenhouse, S. (2003, September 25). Immigrants' rights drive starts. *New York Times.* Retrieved November 4, 2003, from http://www.nytimes.com/2003/09/25/national/25FREE.html?pagewanted=1

Gutkin, T., & Curtis, M. (1999). School-based consultation theory and practice: The art and science of indirect service delivery. In C. R. Reynolds & T. B. Gutkin (Eds.), *The handbook of school psychology, 3rd edition* (pp. 577–613). New York: Wiley.

Hall, C. I. H. (1997). Cultural malpractice: The growing obsolescence of psychology with the changing U.S. population. *American Psychologist, 52,* 642–651.

Hall, E. T. (1976). *Beyond culture.* New York: Anchor.

Helman, C. (1994). *Culture, health and illness* (3rd ed.). London: Butterworth Heineman.

Henning-Stout, M. (1995). *A collaboration project: Mexican migrant families and early childhood education in Yamhill County, Oregon.* Denver, CO: Western Regional Falculty Institute for Training.

Henning-Stout, M. (1996). Que podemos hacer?: Roles for school psychologists with Mexican and Latino migrant children and families. *School Psychology Review, 25,* 152–164.

Huang, L. N., & Gibbs, J. T. (1992). Partners or adversaries? Home–school collaboration across culture, race, and ethnicity. In S. L. Christenson & J. C. Conoley (Eds.), *Home–school collaboration* (pp. 81–109). Bethesda, MD: National Association of School Psychologists.

La Roche, M. J., & Shirberg, D. (2004). High stakes exams and Latino students: Toward a culturally sensitive education for Latino children in the United States. *Journal of Educational and Psychological Consultation, 15,* 205–223.

Lopez, G. R., Scribner, J. D., & Mahitivanichcha, K. (2001). Redefining parental involvement: Lessons from high-performing migrant-impacted schools. *American Educational Research Journal, 38,* 253–288.

Lott, B. (2001). Low-income parents and the public schools. *Journal of Social Issues, 57,* 247–260.

Magana, C. G., & Hovey, J. D. (2003). Psychosocial stressors associated with Mexican migrant farmworkers in the midwest United States. *Journal of Immigrant Health, 5,* 75–86.

Marmot, M. (1999). In M. Marmot & G. Wilkinson (Eds.), *Social determinants of health* . New York: Oxford.

Martinez, Y. G., & Velazquez, J. (2001). *Involving migrant families in education* (Report No. ED448010). Charleston, WV: Clearinghouse on Rural Education & Small Schools. (ERIC Document Reproduction Services No. ED 1.331/2:EDO–RC–00–4)

Merino, B., Trueba, E., & Samaniego, F. (1993). *Language and culture in learning: Teaching Spanish to native speakers of Spanish*. Washington, DC: Falmer.

Mikhail, B. (1994). Hispanic mother's beliefs and practices regarding selected children's health problems. *Western Journal of Nursing Practices, 16,* 623–638.

National Center for Health Services. (2001). Healthy people 2000 final review. (DHHS Publication No. 01.0256). Hyattsville, MD: Public Health Service.

Nuestra Comunidad Sana. (2004). Retrieved January 27, 2004, from http://community.gorge.net/ncs/

Pulaski, A. (2003, September 23). Migrant worker pact reached. *The Oregonian,* pp. A1, A10.

Putnam, R. D., & Feldstein, L. M. (2003). *Better together: Restoring the American community*. New York: Simon & Schuster.

Pyler v. Doe, 457 U. S. 202, 102 S. Ct. 2382 (1982).

Ramos, C. S. (2003). "Estudia para que no te pase lo que a mi": Narrativas culturales sobre el valor de la escuela en familias Mexicanas [Study to avoid what happened to me: Cultural narratives on the value of education in Mexican families]. *Journal of Latinos and Education, 2,* 197–216.

Rogers, M. R. (1998). The influence of race and consultant verbal behavior on perceptions of consultant competence and multicultural sensitivity. *School Psychology Quarterly, 13,* 265–280.

Ruiz-de-Velasco, J., & Fix, M. (2000). *Overlooked & underserved: Immigrant students in U. S. secondary schools*. Washington, DC: The Urban Institute.

Shi, L., & Singh, D. A. (1998). *Delivering health care in America: A systems approach*. Gaithersberg, MD: Aspen.

Stevens, E. (1998). Machismo and marianismo. In M. B. Whiteford & S. Whiteford (Eds.), *Crossing currents: Continuity and change in Latin America* (pp. 125–132). Upper Saddle River, NJ: Prentice Hall.

Suarez-Orozco, C., & Suarez-Orozco, M. (2001). *Children of immigration*. Cambridge, MA: Harvard University Press.

Sue, D. W., & Sue, D. (2003). *Counseling the culturally diverse: Theory and practice* (4th ed.). New York: Wiley.

Thomas, W. P., & Collier, V. (1997). *School effectiveness for language minority students* (National Clearinghouse for Bilingual Education Resource Collection Series, No. 9). Retrieved November 4, 2003, from http://www.ncbe.gwu.edu/ncbepubs/resource/effectiveness/

Torres, J. B., Solberg, S. H., & Carlstrom, A. H. (2002). The myth of sameness among Latino men and their machismo. *American Journal of Orthopsychiatry, 72,* 163–181.

United States Department of Labor. (December, 2000). *The agricultural labor market: Status and recommendations*. Retrieved November 4, 2003, from http://migration.ucdavis.edu/rmn/labor_resources/dec_2000_labor.htm

Valencia, R. R., & Black, M. S. (2002). "Mexican Americans don't value education!"—On the basis of the myth, mythmaking, and debunking. *Journal of Latinos and Education, 1,* 81–103.

Zoucha, R. D. (1998). The experiences of Mexican Americans receiving professional nursing care: An ethnonursing study. *Journal of Transcultural Nursing, 9,* 34–44.

Mary M. Clare is a Professor in the Graduate School at Lewis & Clark College in Portland, Oregon. Her research and scholarship have focused on applications of psychology in schools with particular emphasis on identifying and correcting enculturated systems of oppression. Her book, *Responsive Assessment: A New Way of Thinking About Learning* (1994, Jossey-Bass), is in revision.

Anna Jimenez is a Family Medicine Doctor with the Family Medicine Department at Oregon Health & Science University in Portland, Oregon, where she teaches resident doctors. She also is currently completing a second residency in preventive medicine at Oregon Health and Science University. Her clinic is located at the Public Health Department in Oregon City, Oregon, and her emphasis, besides basic primary care, is on the prenatal care of Hispanic women.

Jennifer McClendon is a Resident in Family Medicine at Oregon Health & Science University in Portland, Oregon. On completing her training, she plans to practice in Indian health. Before receiving her medical education, she was a public school educator who focused on teaching migrant and second-language learners.

JOURNAL OF EDUCATIONAL AND PSYCHOLOGICAL CONSULTATION, *16*(1&2), 113–125

COMMENTARY

School Consultants as Change Agents in Achieving Equity for Families in Public Schools

Bonnie K. Nastasi

Institute for Community Research, Hartford, CT

This commentary summarizes four major themes emerging from this special issue: (a) Consultation with nonmainstream families involves empowering parents to navigate the public education system, integrating cultural considerations into consultation and intervention, and educating families and school personnel; (b) a participatory process that brings together families, school personnel, and community stakeholders is critical to achieving educational equity; (c) a cultural mediator is necessary to assist stakeholders in bridging cultural gaps and achieving shared meanings; and (d) educational equity is a complex, long-term process involving numerous individual, relational, organizational, community, and societal factors. School consultants can play a central role in facilitating inquiry, negotiation, consensus building, and individual and systemic change to achieve cross-cultural collaboration and educational equity.

The articles in this issue provide multiple perspectives on the role of school consultants in facilitating involvement of nonmainstream families in their children's education. The efforts described in these articles repre-

Correspondence should be sent to Bonnie K. Nastasi, PhD, Associate Director of Interventions, Institute for Community Research, 2 Hartford Square West, Suite 100, Hartford, CT 06106–5128. E-mail: bonnastasi@yahoo.com

sent a range of responses to the barriers faced by families with social, cultural, and economic experiences that are different from those of mainstream society as they attempt to access and navigate the public educational system. As the guest editors (Lott & Rogers, this issue) suggest, the task of school consultants is to promote both empowerment of parents as advocates for their children's education and responsiveness of school personnel to parental advocacy and participation. The work of contributing authors provide insights and strategies for those school consultants interested in assuming the role of mediators or negotiators across the cultural boundaries of nonmainstream families and mainstream public education.

The contributors to this issue addressed two key questions: (a) What are the key features of a consultation model for facilitating equity in education for nonmainstream families? (b) How can school consultants best utilize their positions and expertise to enhance the role of nonmainstream parents in public education? The focus of this commentary is to identify the themes that represent answers to these questions across the individual articles and to draw implications of the collective work of the contributors for a general model of consultation with nonmainstream families.

MAJOR THEMES

Four general themes characterize the approaches and issues relevant to involving nonmainstream parents in public education: (a) focus of school consultation; (b) importance of collaboration among stakeholders; (c) need for cultural mediators, facilitators, or brokers to bring together nonmainstream families and mainstream educators; and (d) the mediating factors that facilitate or inhibit nonmainstream parental involvement in education. These themes reflect points of consensus as well as emerging ideas. This section is devoted to describing these themes using examples from the articles in this issue.

Focus of Consultation

Recognizing the general goal as achieving equity in education for nonmainstream families, most of the contributors identified the specific foci of consultation as the following: (a) empowering parents to navigate the public education system, (b) effectively integrating cultural considerations into consultation and intervention efforts, and (c) educating both families and school personnel. The contributors provide multiple perspectives and strategies for addressing these foci across different types of nonmainstream families.

Empowering parents. The primary focus of school consultation with nonmainstream parents is to enhance parental capacity for effectively navigating school systems (Lott & Rogers, this issue). The interpretation of this focus by contributing authors ranged from empowerment of parents as independent agents to structural changes within schools and society. Koonce and Harper (this issue) describe an approach that involved training and supporting parents to access and navigate schools. The school consultant worked in partnership with a community-based organization to prepare African American parents as advocates for their children's education. Parents received training and coaching regarding educational systems and policies, and communicating and negotiating with school personnel. In addition, the project focused on building capacity within the community-based organization to continue these efforts. Guishard et al. (this issue) describe a program for empowering the next generation of parents through work with youth, thus extending the efforts of an existing community activist organization.

Jeltova and Fish (this issue) propose a combination of systemic and traditional consultation to prepare schools to bring about structural changes leading to empowerment of gay, lesbian, bisexual, and transgender (GLBT) parents and their children. They call for schools to become independent agents of change (problem solvers) through structural modifications such as revising school mission, changing discriminatory school policies, educating school personnel, creating safe zones, and making curriculum inclusive of GLBT issues. Similarly, Clare, Jimenez, and McClendon (this issue) call for responsiveness of service providers (consultants, school personnel) to the specific needs and culture of migrant families, thus advocating for structural changes that foster family involvement and empowerment.

Integrating cultural considerations. Evident in all the efforts described in this issue is attention to the "culture" of nonmainstream families, that is, to the shared beliefs, values, language, customs, and norms relevant to the respective nonmainstream group and its families. Each of the contributors calls for consultants to learn about the culture of the specific target group and individual families; explore the potential conflicts between schools, as embodiments of mainstream culture, and nonmainstream families; and consider ways to not only address these conflicts but also to incorporate features (e.g., language, experiences, beliefs) of the nonmainstream culture into consultation efforts.

Guishard et al. (this issue) use a participatory action research process for helping both youth and researchers to understand the intergenerational (youth, parents, grandparents) culture of South Bronx families through the creation of oral histories. Koonce and Harper (this issue) facilitate a collaborative process to provide cross-cultural opportunities for school and community consultants to learn about African American families. Clare et al. (this issue) go beyond mere consideration of cultural perspectives and experiences to advocate for identifying and utilizing the cultural strengths or "wisdom" of nonmainstream individuals (i.e., migrant farm workers) in consultation.

Ochoa and Rhodes (this issue) encourage the application of Ingraham's (2000) multicultural school consultation (MSC) framework that involves explicit focus on the potentially diverse cultures of schools, families, and consultants, and called for professional development of cross-cultural competencies (as proposed by Rogers, 2000) among school consultants. Consultants are expected to maintain "a focus on unique cultural, familial, and experiential perspectives of families and students" (Ochoa & Rhodes, this issue, p. 89), in this case in working with bilingual families.

Multicultural or cross-cultural consultation requires a cultural focus that extends beyond the family and includes understanding the culture of schools and of individual consultants. Jeltova and Fish (this issue), for example, call for understanding and addressing the potentially conflicting cultures of nonmainstream GLBT families and public schools. As they point out, nonmainstream families are likely to have cultural experiences and values that are both consistent with and in conflict with mainstream families and schools. Furthermore, facilitating systemic change in public education requires a thorough understanding of school culture. Achieving educational equity for nonmainstream families thus requires that both nonmainstream families and mainstream school personnel learn about each other. This learning can be facilitated in a number of ways, including education or training, direct interaction, and mediation or brokering by a third party. Each of the mechanisms is explored in subsequent sections.

Education of both families and school personnel.   All the contributors stress the importance of educating both family members and school personnel. As Lott and Rogers (this issue) point out, parents who are not at ease and feel unwelcome in the schools are at a disadvantage when advocating for their children's educational needs. In addition, lack of knowledge contributes to stereotyping and negative attitudes toward nonmainstream families among school personnel. Jeltova and Fish (this issue) describe a process for cognitive change among school personnel that involves confronting misconceptions and dispelling myths about GLBT families through in-service training. Koonce and Harper (this issue) describe a training program that provides parents with information about the political and cultural environment of public education to prepare them to better navigate school systems on behalf of their children. Clare et al. (this issue) provide several examples of strategies for educating school personnel about migrant Latino families, including presentations by cultural experts and encouraging families to share their cultural experiences through storytelling. Guishard and her colleagues (this issue) use participatory action research as a mechanism for cultural learning.

In addition to cultural considerations, the contributors emphasize the importance of knowledge about specific educational issues that face nonmainstream students and their families, and provide readers with a review of these issues. For example, Lott and Rogers (this issue) review empirical evidence on the barriers to educational success for nonmainstream students. Jeltova and Fish (this issue) provide information from research about GLBT families, their experiences with discrimination, and school factors that contribute to inequities for GLBT students and children of GLBT parents. Clare and her colleagues (this issue) describe the experiences and culture of Mexican migrant families. Ochoa and Rhodes (this issue) review research on the relative effectiveness of different approaches to bilingual education that can assist both parents and school personnel in decision making.

In summary, there is consensus among the contributors regarding the critical foci of consultation with nonmainstream parents, that is, empowerment of parents and schools to bring about change, incorporating cultural considerations into consultation and intervention, and providing opportunities for families and school personnel to learn about each other through education and training. In the next section, direct interaction is explored as another mechanism for facilitating cross-cultural understanding.

Collaboration Among Stakeholders

A critical component of the approaches described in this issue is a collaborative or participatory process in which members of mainstream school and nonmainstream family cultures work together to address educational inequity. Engaging parents in a collaborative problem-solving process with school personnel is viewed as a mechanism for parental empowerment, addressing cultural barriers, mutual understanding, and educational change. Jeltova and Fish (this issue), for example, discuss the importance of improving communication between school personnel and families and facilitating school–family collaboration within the context of organizational or individual or small group consultation.

Contributors also stress the importance of involving community stakeholders in facilitating school–family partnerships or parental empowerment. Koonce and Harper (this issue) describe a program in Rhode Island that capitalizes on the existing relationships between families and a community organization to bring together schools and families. Employing this three-way partnership, school consultants can help to establish a sustainable process for parental empowerment through a trusted and established community-based organization. Guishard and colleagues (this issue) build on previously successful efforts of an existing grassroots organization to extend the role of families and community members in addressing educational inequity. Guishard et al. also extend stakeholder participation to include youth and university researchers with the goal of building capacity for youth to conduct research for the purpose of social change such as achieving educational equity.

Consistent with an ecological perspective, focused on multiple contexts in which the child lives and multiple influences on the child's life, Clare and her colleagues (this issue) advocate for extending the key stakeholder groups to include those that address health and social service needs of children and families. Arguing for responsive consultation and education, Clare et al. suggest the inclusion of professionals from multiple disciplines (e.g., nursing, public health, social work, education) in efforts to both understand and address educational inequities among migrant families. For example, successful involvement of parents in children's education may require reducing domestic workloads (e.g., providing child care) and providing transportation to school meetings. In addition, difficulties in accessing and navigating educational systems parallel the difficulties these families experience with regard to health care. Thus, educators and health care providers might work together in identifying ways to improve access and utilization.

Central to effective involvement of nonmainstream families is communication across cultural barriers, particularly those that separate nonmainstream families from mainstream public education. Even when collaboration among stakeholders was not an explicit focus, this issue's contributors emphasized the importance of improving communication between mainstream school personnel and nonmainstream parents. Furthermore, contributors examined the role of a third party such as the school consultant in facilitating the interaction between families and schools.

Cultural Mediator, Facilitator, or Broker

A consistent theme across all the articles in this issue is necessity of a mediator, facilitator, or broker to bridge the cultural gap between mainstream schools and nonmainstream families. Contributors agreed that school consultants are in ideal positions to assume the responsibility of cultural mediator. Lott and Rogers (this issue), for example, describe school consultants as agents of change for both parents and school personnel, facilitating empowerment of parents and responsiveness of school personnel so that both parties are prepared to engage in negotiation across cultural differences. Similarly, Jeltova and Fish (this issue) assign school consultants the responsibility for empowering relevant stakeholders and facilitating collaboration between mainstream schools (or specific school personnel) and nonmainstream GLBT families.

The role of mediator also can be assumed by community consultants. For example, Koonce and Harper (this issue) describe a program in which a consultant located within a community-based organization works with families and with school consultants to mediate cultural differences between African American families and mainstream schools. University researchers Guishard et al. (this issue) served as consultants to assist a community activist organization in efforts to promote parental empowerment and involvement in education. If positioned within established and respected community-based organizations, community consultants can contribute to sustainability of educational equity efforts. In both of these programs, specific attention was given to capacity building within the existing organization so that parental involvement efforts could persist without external efforts (e.g., beyond the involvement of university researchers).

Although either school or community consultants can help to facilitate school–family alliances, in some instances, their limited experiences with family or school culture can preclude effective mediation. The school consultant must be knowledgeable about the culture of the mainstream school, the culture of the nonmainstream family, and the educational issues faced by specific nonmainstream groups. To work effectively with the nonmainstream families represented in this issue (bilingual, African American, GLBT, migrant Mexican, and low income) as well as the diverse families within multicultural urban communities, school consultants must have a vast range of cultural and empirical knowledge. Alternatively, consultants can enlist the help of individuals who are knowledgeable about respective nonmainstream groups and issues (i.e., cultural brokers, Ochoa & Rhodes, this issue; community advocates, Clare et al., this issue). Just as language interpreters can assist consultants in communicating with non-English-speaking families (Lopez, 2000), "cultural interpreters" (brokers or advocates) can assist consultants in communicating with families who represent nonmainstream cultures (Nastasi, Varjas, Bernstein, & Jayasena, 2000).

The role of the school consultant extends beyond the facilitation of school–family alliances to include monitoring and addressing the myriad factors that can facilitate or impede nonmainstream parental involvement and educational equity for nonmainstream students. Attending to the factors that mediate school–family collaboration and involving key stakeholders in capitalizing on facilitators and reducing inhibitors are critical aspects of the consultant's role. Mediating factors identified by the contributing authors are described in the next section.

Mediating Factors

Perhaps the best way to conceptualize the factors that facilitate or inhibit educational equity for nonmainstream families is within an ecological framework. These factors occur at individual, relational, organizational, community, and societal levels, necessitating monitoring and intervention at multiple levels. At the individual stakeholder level, cross-cultural knowledge and experiences, prejudicial attitudes, and communication and negotiation skills can foster or inhibit educational equity and parental involvement (see Clare et al., this issue; Jeltova & Fish, this issue; Koonce & Harper, this issue; Lott & Rogers, this issue). At the relational level, prior experiences of families (individually or collectively) with school personnel and community organizations can influence responsiveness of stakeholders to engage in collaborative efforts (Koonce & Harper, this issue; Lott & Rogers, this issue).

Institutional and social policies and practices (e.g., antigay harassment policies, bilingual education programming, flexibility in curriculum to address nonmainstream issues) can pose barriers or mechanisms to facilitate involvement of nonmainstream parents (Clare et al., this issue;

Jeltova & Fish, this issue; Ochoa & Rhodes, this issue). The availability of resources and prior experiences with political advocacy within extended family, community organizations, and social networks can operate at the community level (Clare et al., this issue; Guishard et al., this issue; Koonce & Harper, this issue). For example, Guishard et al. (this issue) capitalized on prior successes of parents within a community-based organization in advocating for school reform as the basis for building community capacity. Similarly, Koonce and Harper (this issue) utilized the resources of an existing community-based organization to facilitate parental empowerment and school–family alliances. The prejudices and myths that impede cross-cultural collaboration within schools are reflected also in the larger society (Jeltova & Fish, this issue; Lott & Rogers, this issue). Furthermore, social issues such as poverty and availability of affordable child care can influence the feasibility of nonmainstream parental involvement in education (Clare et al., this issue).

Finally, these mediating factors operate in a dynamic and synergistic way to influence nonmainstream parental involvement in education. The role of the school consultant is to assess these factors, identify targets for intervention, and make use of existing resources to bring about change at individual, relational, organizational, community, and societal levels. The contributors to this issue present examples of consultation models and strategies to guide the school consultant's work with an array of nonmainstream families. The perspectives and experiences represented in this issue also move us toward a model of consultation for facilitating equity across diverse cultures, which is consistent with current approaches to multicultural, cross-cultural, or culture-specific consultation.

MOVING TOWARD A MODEL OF CONSULTATION FOR FACILITATING EQUITY

The purpose of this issue was to address two main questions: What are the key features of a consultation model for facilitating equity in education for nonmainstream families? And, how can school consultants best utilize their positions and expertise to enhance the role of nonmainstream parents in public education? The answers to these questions provide the basis for conceptualizing a consultation model for working with nonmainstream families. This section is devoted to summarizing the major themes of this issue with reference to the two questions and current models of multicultural consultation.

What Are the Key Features of a Consultation Model for Facilitating Equity in Education for Nonmainstream Families?

The contributing authors describe models and strategies for consultation with specific nonmainstream populations. The themes emerging from their collective efforts provide the basis for a general consultation model for working with nonmainstream families which is consistent with models of multicultural consultation such as MSC (Ingraham, 2000), Multicultural Conjoint Behavioral Consultation (Sheridan, 2000), Participatory Culture-Specific Consultation (PCSC; Nastasi et al., 2000), and a systemic model for cross-cultural consultation (Maital, 2000). Based on the work represented in this issue, the following features of a multicultural model for nonmainstream families are proposed:

1. Promoting equity in education requires individual and systemic change for all stakeholder groups (e.g., parents, teachers, administrators, policymakers). A primary focus in consultation with nonmainstream families is the empowerment of individuals (e.g., parents, teachers, community members) and systems (e.g., schools, families, community organizations) to effect such changes.

2. Mutual understanding and integration of cultural perspectives and experiences of nonmainstream parents and mainstream educators are prerequisites for achieving equity. Participatory (collaborative) approaches provide the opportunities for gaining cross-cultural knowledge and developing shared perspectives. Cultural brokers, with cross-cultural expertise and mediation skills, can facilitate communication across mainstream and nonmainstream boundaries.

3. Individual, relational, organizational, community, and societal factors can operate individually or synergistically as facilitators or inhibitors to achieving and sustaining equity. Effective consultation requires an ecological model to guide assessment and intervention across these multiple levels.

4. Achieving educational equity for nonmainstream families requires consideration of the family constellation within their ecological niche and attention to personal, economic, and social needs. Understanding the lives of nonmainstream families and addressing the myriad needs is best achieved through interdisciplinary and interagency partnerships.

5. Formal and informal community groups (e.g., community-based organizations, grassroots advocacy groups, neighborhood networks) represent critical and sustainable links to nonmainstream families. Establishing

partnerships with these groups can facilitate understanding, access, and involvement of families. Moreover, community groups provide important mechanisms for sustaining change efforts.

Inherent in the work of this issue's contributing authors and in existing multicultural consultation models (e.g., MSC, PCSC) is the central role of culture—the culture of clients, consultees, and consultants who are embedded in ecological systems. Culture is considered critical to understanding the needs and resources within each stakeholder group. Culture influences the beliefs, values, and behaviors of clients, consultees, and consultants, the interactions among these stakeholders as they engage in consultation, and the conceptualization of target problems and solutions. Culture is an important consideration regardless of the model of consultation (e.g., behavioral, mental health). Moreover, negotiating cultural differences and appreciating cultural similarities are essential to successful consultation, especially when attempting to work across mainstream and nonmainstream boundaries (e.g., involving nonmainstream families in mainstream public education). Finally, the consultant plays a key role in negotiating these cultural differences.

How Can School Consultants Best Utilize Their Positions and Expertise to Enhance the Role of Nonmainstream Parents in Public Education?

The themes from this issue guide the delineation of responsibilities and expertise for school consultants who are interested in applying a multicultural consultation model. School consultants are viewed as change agents or facilitators of collaboration and shared problem solving among stakeholders (e.g., parents, teachers, school administrators). The consultant's responsibilities include identifying stakeholders, providing necessary education and training, guiding the participatory process, and enlisting the help of others with cultural knowledge, professional expertise, or links to community. Consultants are expected to utilize their knowledge of educational systems and policies, interpersonal and consultation skills, and assessment and intervention skills to facilitate reciprocal learning of culture, participatory problem solving, data collection, and design, implementation, and evaluation of interventions.

Assuming the role of multicultural consultant requires rethinking traditional notions of consultation and developing competencies that go beyond traditional assessment, consultation, and intervention skills.

Definitions of cultural competencies have been presented elsewhere (e.g., American Psychological Association, 1993; Campinha-Bacote, 2002; Leong & Wong, 2003; Nastasi et al., 2000; Rogers, 2000; Sue, 2001) and reflect a range of definitions. Inherent across these multiple perspectives are the following essential competencies: (a) self-reflection about one's own cultural experiences and belief system, (b) willingness to consider diverse viewpoints and learn from others, (c) understanding of the role of culture in human development (e.g., ecological perspective), (d) culture-specific knowledge (e.g., knowledge about specific cultural groups), (e) inquiry skills such as ethnographic or qualitative research methods, and (f) a communication style characterized by negotiation and consensus building. The capacity to engage others across cultural boundaries might best be described as co-constructive, characterized by an interpersonal style that involves eliciting and contemplating multiple perspectives, and negotiating across divergent views to reach shared understanding. Thus, cultural competence is more indicative of a way of viewing the world and interacting with others rather than a set of discrete skills.

Working with nonmainstream families poses both opportunities and challenges. School consultants bring to the task a unique combination of skills that are critical for engaging in inquiry, negotiating across divergent worldviews, and facilitating the co-construction of solutions for educational equity. Achieving equity in education for nonmainstream families involves challenging established mainstream practices and beliefs, crossing deep-rooted cultural boundaries, and overcoming institutional barriers. This endeavor requires the concerted efforts of multiple players. School consultants cannot achieve equity alone but are in the position to facilitate cross-cultural partnerships and to orchestrate social and cultural change.

REFERENCES

American Psychological Association. (1993). Guidelines for providers of psychological services to ethnic, linguistic, and culturally diverse populations. *American Psychologist, 48,* 45–48.

Campinha-Bacote, J. (2002). The process of cultural competence in the delivery of health care services: A model of care. *Journal of Transcultural Nursing, 13,* 181–184.

Ingraham, C. L. (2000). Consultation through a multicultural lens: Multicultural and cross-cultural consultation in schools. *School Psychology Review, 29,* 320–343.

Leong, F. T., & Wong, P. T. (2003). Optimal human functioning from cross-cultural perspectives: Cultural competence as an organizing framework. In W. B. Walsh (Ed.), *Counseling* psychology and optimal human functioning: Contemporary topics in vocational psychology (pp. 123–150). Mahwah, NJ: Lawrence Erlbaum Associates, Inc.

Lopez, E. C. (2000). Conducting instructional consultation through interpreters. School Psychology Review, 29, 378–388.

Maital, S. L. (2000). Reciprocal distancing: A systems model of interpersonal processes in cross-cultural consultation. School Psychology Review, 29, 389–400.

Nastasi, B. K., Varjas, K., Bernstein, R., & Jayasena, A. (2000). Conducting participatory culture-specific consultation: A global perspective on multicultural consultation. School Psychology Review, 29, 401–413.

Rogers, M. R. (2000). Examining the cultural context of consultation. School Psychology Review, 29, 414–418.

Sheridan, S. M. (2000). Considerations of multiculturalism and diversity in behavioral consultation with parents and teachers. School Psychology Review, 29, 344–353.

Sue, D. W. (2001). Multidimensional facets of cultural competence. Counseling Psychologist, 29, 790–821.

Bonnie K. Nastasi, PhD (Kent State University, 1986), is now at Walden University, Minneapolis, MN, as Director of School Psychology. She is former Associate Director of Interventions at the Institute for Community Research. She has conducted applied research on mental health and health risk among school-age and adult populations in the United States and Asia. Her interests include mental health promotion, health risk prevention, use of qualitative research methods in psychology, and promoting school psychology internationally. She has coauthored two books, School-Based Mental Health Programs: Creating Comprehensive and Culturally Specific Mental Health Programs (2004; coauthors, Rachel Bernstein Moore and Kristen Varjas; American Psychological Association), and School Interventions for Children of Alcoholics (1994; coauthor, Denise M. DeZolt; Guilford Press). Dr. Nastasi has served as Associate Editor for School Psychology Review and School Psychology Quarterly.

www.ingramcontent.com/pod-product-compliance
Ingram Content Group UK Ltd.
Pitfield, Milton Keynes, MK11 3LW, UK
UKHW020422010325
455677UK00029B/973